SOJOURNER TRUTH

SOJOURNER TRUTH

A Biography

Larry G. Murphy

GREENWOOD BIOGRAPHIES

 GREENWOOD

AN IMPRINT OF ABC-CLIO, LLC
Santa Barbara, California • Denver, Colorado • Oxford, England

Library of Congress Cataloging-in-Publication Data

Murphy, Larry G. (Larry George), 1946–
  Sojourner Truth : a biography / Larry G. Murphy.
    p. cm. — (Greenwood biographies)
  Includes bibliographical references and index.
    ISBN 978-0-313-35728-2 (acid-free paper) — ISBN 978-0-313-35729-9
(ebook)   1. Truth, Sojourner, d. 1883.   2. African American abolitionists—
Biography.   3. African American women—Biography.   4. Abolitionists—
United States—Biography.   5. Social reformers—United States—
Biography.   I. Title.
    E185.97.T8M87   2011
    305.5'67092—dc22
    [B]   2010040839

ISBN: 978-0-313-35728-2
EISBN: 978-0-313-35729-9

15   14   13   12   11   1   2   3   4   5

This book is also available on the World Wide Web as an eBook.
Visit www.abc-clio.com for details.

Greenwood
An Imprint of ABC-CLIO, LLC

ABC-CLIO, LLC
130 Cremona Drive, P.O. Box 1911
Santa Barbara, California 93116-1911

This book is printed on acid-free paper (∞)
Manufactured in the United States of America

I dedicate this work to my four sisters—Marian, Lora, Beverly, and Carol, women of strength, competence, high moral character, and self-giving commitment to things that truly matter

CONTENTS

ACKNOWLEDGMENTS

I want to acknowledge the contributions to this work of several persons, agencies, and sources, without which it would not have come to be. First is Barbara Fears, my research assistant, who patiently gathered and efficiently organized the great majority of the print and Internet resource documents upon which this writing was based. Second is Carleton Mabee and daughter Susan Mabee Newhouse, whose meticulously researched and critically presented biography, *Sojourner Truth: Slave, Prophet, Legend,* was an invaluable resource in constructing my own rendition of the story.

I am also indebted to Erlene Stetson and Linda David for the insights on the life of Sojourner Truth offered in their thoughtful volume *Glorying in Tribulation: The Lifework of Sojourner Truth.* In this same regard, I lift the name of Margaret Washington, whose critical Introduction to her reprinting of the *Narrative of Sojourner Truth* offered provocative perspectives on our common subject. I acknowledge here the competent guidance to resources extended by George Livingston, librarian at the Willard Library, Helen Warner Branch, Battle Creek, Michigan, as well as the assistance of Mary Butler and the staff of the Sojourner Truth Library/Archive, Battle Creek, and the Periodicals &

Newspapers Reading Room staff at Northwestern University, Evanston, Illinois. Of course, the scholarly and interpretive contributions of many more persons were incorporated in significant ways into the present work, and they are credited in the bibliography.

I thank my institution, Garrett-Evangelical Theological Seminary, for the generous sabbatical leave wherein this writing was accomplished. I thank the editors at ABC-CLIO for the opportunity to undertake this writing project, by which I was greatly enriched, for their patience in seeing it through to completion, and for their skill in bringing it to publishable form.

INTRODUCTION

Once called on very short notice to address an audience, Sojourner Truth was quoted as having said, "Well, chilern, I have come here like the rest of ye, to hear what I have to say." Having something to say, though, was not an issue for this trumpet of often-uncomfortable truth to the citizenry of the 19th-century United States of America, not even on that occasion. Of the many highly reputed, historically significant orators of the day, Sojourner Truth was among the most prolific—and most quoted. Her ability to entrance crowds with pungent, perceptive analysis of the issues at hand and to regale them with powerful singing, including of her own compositions, placed her in demand among the organizers of the major emerging progressive social advocacy movements of her time.

Yet Truth was not a "speaker for hire." The lectures and speeches she gave, whether by invitation or at her own scheduling, were, like her singing, nonremunerated, genuine implementations of a life mission, grounded in a deeply convicted religious faith. "Truth burns up error," was a phrase she once used, not referring to herself but to the message she felt impelled to deliver. It reflected her conviction that her God, the God of her unique vision of Christian faith, had commissioned

her to inject a prophetic word of justice into the oppressive, ineq-
uitable social practices that enthralled persons across boundaries of
racial, gender, ethnic, and social class identities. For Truth, these were
not separate issues to be addressed seriatim but were simply different
faces of the same mandate for inclusive human community founded in
nondiscriminatory justice, universal human rights, and mutual respect
in social relationships, as manifestations of her God's cosmic, all-
encompassing love.

For nearly 40 years, Sojourner Truth traversed the states of the North,
East, and Midwest, speaking to public assemblies, large and small. What
began as a religious, evangelistic undertaking transitioned into a faith-
directed social-reform mission that found specific, concrete focus on
a number of causes, primarily the abolition of slavery, equal rights for
women, temperance, and—after Emancipation—material and social
service supports for the now-free black population to move into secure,
self-supporting, responsible citizenship. Since she always understood
these efforts as merely the working out of a divine calling for social
"redemption," her speeches were interspersed with biblical quotes, par-
ables, and religious references, and typically accompanied at some point
with the singing of sacred songs. A "sojourner" on the road, she relied
on the hospitality of friends and strangers and the sale her biography
and photographs of herself to support her needs. In her reform efforts,
she partnered with many of the most prominent names in the 19th century, from Frederick Douglass, William Lloyd Garrison, Elizabeth Cady
Stanton, and Susan B. Anthony to Wendell Phillips, Horace Greeley,
Frances Ellen Watkins Harper, Bishop Daniel Payne, and several others
of lesser name recognition but of substantial historical significance.

Such a life narrative is made particularly notable by the fact that its
subject, celebrated for her public speaking and astute social analysis,
remained illiterate for all of her approximately 86 years of life. With
never a day of formal schooling, she could neither read nor write and
depended on her grandsons and on trusted friends to read for her and to
write letters and other communications. This was a practice commonly
used by persons of the time. Later generations, then, are dependent on
these persons, on journalistic media reports of her speeches, and on the
printed recollections of those who personally interacted with her, for
the record of her thoughts and words.

Because Truth's words were thus mediated through the pens of others, we have a "filtered" vista into who she was. There is sufficiently broad corroboration and overlap in the reporting on what she said that the fundamental content seems reliably to have been retained. For instance, whether her famous reply to Frederick Douglass's pessimism about the prospects for enslaved blacks' nonviolent address to their predicament was "Frederick, is God dead?" or, as some have reconstructed the evidence, "Frederick, is God gone?," the point is the same, and the impact in the historical situation is confirmed by all the data from the time.

How Truth expressed herself—her grammar, diction, and idiom—has also been filtered, consciously and unconsciously, by those who reported on her words. Some of the filtering resulted from the association in the American mind between the institution of slavery and the geographic South, where it was predominantly practiced. Abolition, and the reform movement associated with it, portrayed the subjects of its advocacy efforts with the characteristics of the southern black cultural context. Sojourner Truth, however, was among those enslaved in the North, in many ways a differentiated venue. In the South, blacks lived and labored in situations where there were concentrations of blacks, often 20 or more on a farm. The composite black community across the region, numbering ultimately in the millions, developed a distinct social, religious, and linguistic culture. In the North, on the other hand, the enslaved numbered in the year 1800 only some 40,000, and that number was declining.

This relatively small number across the region, living in much greater isolation from one another, had far less opportunity to develop and transmit a distinct, fully articulated black cultural complex. For instance, in rural New York, where Sojourner Truth was born in the late 18th century, blacks were widely dispersed, typically with only one or two enslaved blacks living with a Dutch family. And while the commonalities of the condition of enslavement, including the deprivations and cruelties found in all regions, would generate similar creative communal survival and self-actualization responses, the regional particularities of these would be different from those in the South, under these differing circumstances. And so, Truth loved participating in the Pinkster festival, a Dutch celebration of Pentecost not familiar to southern blacks. And she grew through her juvenile years speaking only Dutch. Thus, one must take caution when Truth's words are rendered in the grammar and idioms typical of southern blacks.

Truth was an exemplar for white abolitionists of the worthy personhood of the enslaved African, whom they were trying to redeem from chatteldom. Her account of her enslavement was of the poignant, wrenching mode that they wanted to project to the world as compelling support for their case. There was a tendency, then, for sympathetic whites, consciously or carelessly, to portray her and reframe her words in the mold of the black of the South, the stereotypical venue of the enslaved. But a member of the Dumont family, to which she was last enslaved, said that Truth definitely did not speak in whites' construction of black southern dialect. Truth herself was aware of this linguistic portrayal and objected to its inaccuracy. Growing into full adulthood, Truth eventually came to speak fluent English, an accomplishment in which she took pride. Nonetheless, she, like many, if not most, "second language" speakers, retained her "accent" (Dutch, in this case) and the use of certain words and idiomatic expressions from her earliest days. Thus, when the text of the present work quotes passages attributed to Truth, the language will be rendered in standard English, except where it appears to the author that the grammar and word choices would likely have been those Truth actually would have employed.

Sojourner Truth rose from slavery to become one of the nation's most widely recognized and renowned figures. She lived a long life, with a flourish of activity for social and political justice almost to the very end. In challenging the laws and customs of her day, she charted many firsts for African Americans and for women. As legend, and biographers' faulty documentation, came to attribute much-elevated years to her lifespan—20 more years than records can substantiate—she eventually went along with the fiction, perhaps believing it to be so. She did not know her actual year of birth, though for her that date was not significant. She marked her "birth" year as 1843, the year she left behind her former life as Isabella Van Wagenen and began her mission as Sojourner Truth. And in the absence of an actual birth *day*, she came finally to adopt Christmas as the day to celebrate it.

Sojourner Truth's story provides a revealing window into much of the interior life of the 19th-century United States—its mores and values; its degrading social practices and redeeming social graces; its hopes, fears, and, as Truth would have claimed, its possibilities for being a place where the best of human striving could be fulfilled.

TIMELINE: EVENTS IN THE LIFE OF SOJOURNER TRUTH

ca. 1797   Isabella is born into slavery on the Johannes Hardenbergh estate, Swartekill, at Stone Ridge, Town of Hurley, Ulster County, New York.

ca. 1799   Isabella is inherited by Charles Hardenbergh, son of Johannes.

ca. 1806   Isabella is bought at auction for $100 by John Neely, of Twaalfskill, near Kingston, New York. She remembered being about nine years old.

ca. 1808   Isabella is bought for $105 by Martinus Schryver of Port Ewen, Kingston, New York. She remembered staying there about 18 months.

1810   Isabella is bought for $175 by John Dumont, of New Paltz, New York. Dumont gives her to marry Thomas, also enslaved to him, with whom she was to bear five children: Diana (1815), Peter (1822), Elizabeth (1825), and Sophia (1826). There are references in the records to a fifth child, possibly named Thomas or Hannah, who may have died in infancy.

Late 1826   Isabella walks to freedom, taking along her infant daughter, Sophia.

July 4, 1827   New York State law grants immediate emancipation to all enslaved persons born before 1799 and gradual emancipation to all the enslaved born after 1799.

1827–28   Isabella is purchased by Isaac and Maria Van Wagenen, in Wagondale, Ulster County, New York, with whom she had taken up residence, in order to prevent her re-enslavement to Dumont. The Van Wagenens employ her for about one year.

Isabella brings a successful, unprecedented lawsuit to recover son Peter, who had been illegally sold into slavery in Alabama.

Isabella moves to Kingston, New York and is employed as a domestic. She has a Christian conversion experience, joining a Methodist church.

1829   Isabella moves, with son Peter, to New York City. She takes work as a domestic and joins John Street Methodist Church.

1831   Isabella works as a domestic for Elijah Pierson, who is advancing some nonmainstream Christian beliefs.

1832–34   Isabella joins Pierson and others in the residential community (the "Kingdom") of Robert Matthews, also known as the Prophet Matthias, located first in New York City, then near Sing Sing, New York.

1834–35   Kingdom dissolves after Prophet Matthias is arrested and tried for the death of Pierson. Isabella is implicated, but she enters and wins a slander suit.

1836–38   Isabella lives again in New York City, working as a domestic. She contends with son Peter's run-ins with the law.

1839   A chance acquaintance of Peter arranges for his employment on a whaling ship, *Zone*, of Nantucket. Peter ships out and writes three letters to Isabella.

1842   The whaler *Zone* returns, but Peter is not on board. Isabella does not hear from him again.

1843   Isabella, at age 46, takes the name Sojourner Truth and leaves New York City, going eastward, to begin a mission as a traveling evangelist. She journeys through New York and Connecticut.

Grandson James Caldwell is born; he would later be one of her traveling companions.

1844–45 Sojourner Truth lives and works at the utopian Northampton Association of Education and Industry, in Northampton, Massachusetts. She meets the anti-slavery and women's rights reformers Giles Stebbins, Wendell Phillips, William Lloyd Garrison, Parker Pillsbury, and Frederick Douglass; she also meets Olive Gilbert, an abolitionist and feminist who would later write the first Truth biography, *Narrative of Sojourner Truth*.

1846 The Northampton Association, unsuccessful in fulfilling its mission, disbands.

1847 George Benson, brother-in-law of William Lloyd Garrison, employs Truth as domestic in his home in Northampton.

1849 Sojourner Truth visits former owner John Dumont; she receives a letter from her daughter Diana.
Truth speaks at American Anti-Slavery Society meeting, May 6–7, in New York City.

1850 Samuel Hill builds and sells a house in Northampton to Isabella Van Wagenen, "sometimes called Sojourner Truth," for a $300 mortgage.
Narrative of Sojourner Truth is published by Olive Gilbert, with preface by William Lloyd Garrison.
In October, Truth speaks at a Women's Rights Convention in Worcester, Massachusetts.
In November, Truth speaks in Providence, Rhode Island, at Fifteenth Annual Meeting of the Rhode Island State Anti-Slavery Society.
In December, Truth speaks at the Old Colony Anti-Slavery Society meeting.

1851 Sojourner Truth joins the speaker's group of abolitionist George Thompson and lectures against slavery in western New York; she travels to Rochester, New York, where she meets and stays with Amy Post, abolitionist and Underground Railroad leader, and speaks in March at Anti-Slavery Convention, Rochester.
In May, Truth attends a Women's Rights Convention in Akron, Ohio, led by prominent activist Frances Dana Gage; here, Truth delivers the famous "Ain't I a Woman" speech.

1851–53   Living in Salem, Ohio, Truth travels the state as an antislavery speaker and works closely with Ohio *Anti-Slavery Bugle* editor Marius Robinson.

1852   In August, she attends the Tenth Annual Meeting of the Western Anti-Slavery Society, in Salem, Ohio, in which she responds to Frederick Douglass, asking "Is God Dead?"

Truth pays off her Northampton mortgage with proceeds from the sale of her biography and photographic *cartes de visite*.

1853   In October, Truth speaks at a suffragist convention at Broadway Tabernacle, New York City, dubbed the "mob convention" because of the disruptive, hostile behaviors of opponents in attendance.

Truth visits Harriet Beecher Stowe in Andover, Massachusetts, traveling with her grandson James Caldwell.

Truth lectures in Williamsburg, New York, and in New York City.

1854   Truth lectures at the American Anti-Slavery Celebration, Framington, Massachusetts.

1855   Truth lectures at the Anti-Slavery Convention, Ashtabula County, Ohio.

The second edition of *Narrative of Sojourner Truth* is published; Harriet Beecher Stowe pens the introduction.

1856   Sojourner Truth is invited by Quaker Henry Willis to Battle Creek, Michigan, to address the Friends of Human Progress convention.

1857   Truth sells her Northampton property and uses the proceeds of the sale to purchase a house and lot in Harmonia, a Spiritualist community six miles west of Battle Creek, Michigan.

1858   Truth visits African Methodist Episcopal (AME) Bishop Daniel Payne in Ohio.

At an October meeting in Silver Lake, Indiana, a hostile audience member accuses her of being a man in disguise; Truth bares her breast to the audience to rebuke the accuser.

1859   Truth is in Detroit, Michigan, for several months.

1860   According to Calhoun County records, residing with Sojourner Truth in her Harmonia home are daughter

Elizabeth Banks, age 35, and grandsons Sammy Banks, age 8, and James "Colvin" (Caldwell), age 16.

1861 Truth gives an antislavery lecture at Angola, Indiana, and is arrested for her protection against the threatening audience.

1862 Sculptor William Wetmore Story is awarded a prize at the London World Exhibition for his statue *Libyan Sibyl*, which was inspired by Harriet Beecher Stowe's recounting to him of Sojourner Truth's life.

1863 Taken ill for several weeks, Truth is given lodging and care in the Battle Creek home of Charles Merritt, prominent citizen and abolitionist, for whom she sometimes worked. A friend writes letter appealing for funds on her behalf, which appears in the *Anti-Slavery Standard*, resulting in many donations.

The April issue of *Atlantic Monthly* magazine carries Harriet Beecher Stowe's article "The Libyan Sibyl," expanding Truth's public recognition.

Truth's grandson James Caldwell enlists in the 54th Regiment, Massachusetts Volunteers (the regiment celebrated in the film *Glory*).

In November, Truth collects food donations in Battle Creek to take Thanksgiving dinner to the black soldiers stationed at Camp Ward in Detroit.

1864 In June, Truth and 13-year-old grandson Sammy Banks travel to Detroit, Michigan, New York, and New Jersey, heading ultimately for Washington, D.C., where they arrive in the fall.

In October, Truth is granted an audience with President Abraham Lincoln at the White House.

The National Freedman's Relief Association deploys Truth's services to address various needs of freedpersons living in settlement camps around Washington.

1864–1867 Truth works at the Freedmen's Hospital in Washington and the Freedmen's Village in Arlington, Virginia and campaigns for the resettlement of freedpersons from camps in the District of Columbia to permanent homes and jobs.

Truth challenges the racial segregation practices of the Washington streetcars and initiates actions that contribute to their desegregation.

1866   Susan B. Anthony, assistant editor of the *National Antislavery Standard*, asks Truth to find a congressperson to present a feminist petition.

1867   Truth makes three trips from Rochester, New York, to the South to resettle freedpersons from there to Rochester.

In May, Truth is the houseguest of Elizabeth Cady Stanton in New York and speaks at First Annual Meeting of the American Equal Rights Association.

Truth moves from Harmonia into Battle Creek, purchasing and beginning the conversion of Merritt "barn" on College Street into her house.

1868   Truth travels to Detroit, then takes a fall speaking tour of western New York state; she tells Amy Post she has succeeded in her effort to quit smoking.

1869   Truth speaks in Pennsylvania, New York, and New Jersey.

1870   County records indicate that living with Truth in her College Street home are her daughter Elizabeth Boyd and husband William, their eight-year-old son William, and Truth's 19-year-old grandson Sammy Banks. Truth's eldest daughter, Diana Corbin, her husband Jacob, and their nine-year-old son Frank are also living in Battle Creek, on South Street, near Oak Hill Cemetery.

Truth embarks on a lecture tour in New Jersey and New York, and in New England. She speaks at the American Woman Suffrage Association meeting; delivers other speeches against alcohol, tobacco, and fashionable dress; and initiates her lectures promoting a petition to resettle freedpersons on government land in the West.

Truth is given an audience with President Ulysses S. Grant at the White House and visits the U.S. Senate chamber, receiving signatures from several senators in her *Book of Life*.

1871   Truth resumes lecturing through New England and New York, receives Frederick Douglass's signature in her *Book of Life*, and speaks in Boston at the Commemoration of the Eighth Anniversary of Negro Freedom in the United States.

In East Saginaw, Michigan, Truth speaks on Spiritualism; in Detroit, she visits friend Nanette Gardner, the first woman to vote in a statewide Michigan election; Gardner notes this in signing Truth's *Book of Life*.

In September, Truth travels to Kansas with grandson Sammy Banks to undertake a speaking tour promoting resettlement of black District of Columbia camp dwellers in the West.

1872   Truth speaks around Kansas, Iowa, Missouri, Wisconsin, Ohio, Indiana, Illinois, and Michigan, then returns to Battle Creek to celebrate the 33rd anniversary of "Emancipation Day" in the British West Indies.

Truth campaigns for the reelection of U.S. Grant but is turned away at the polling place in Battle Creek when she attempts to vote.

1873   Truth visits various cities in Michigan and speaks in New York at the Cooper Institute.

1874   In spring, Truth leaves, with grandson Sammy Banks, for Washington, D.C.; in late fall she is forced to return to Battle Creek when Sammy falls ill; during the winter, Truth herself is taken ill with an ulcer on her leg.

1875   Sammy Banks dies and is buried at Oak Hill Cemetery.

The third edition of the *Narrative* is published, including the *Book of Life*, by friend Frances Titus of Battle Creek.

1876   Truth's health improves, but a relapse causes cancellation of trip to the Centennial celebration in Philadelphia.

1877–78   Truth travels around Michigan with Frances Titus, speaking on temperance.

1878–79   Sojourner Truth and Frances Titus go on a six-month speaking tour through New York and other eastern states.

1879   In August, Truth leaves for Kansas to observe the situation of the "Exodusters," blacks who have emigrated from the South to Kansas; she lectures, en route, in Illinois and Wisconsin, in favor of free government land for formerly enslaved District of Columbia camp dwellers; she works through the fall with Titus and friends Laura Haviland and Elizabeth Comstock to assist in meeting the needs of emigrants.

1880–82　Truth lectures in Michigan, Indiana, and Illinois, advocating temperance and speaking against capital punishment.

1883　In Battle Creek, Truth continues to suffer with ulcers on her legs and is treated by Dr. John Harvey Kellogg of the Battle Creek Sanitarium, who reportedly grafted of some of his own skin onto Truth's leg; she is attended upon her return home by sanitarium medical staff.

November 26, Sojourner Truth dies at her home, 10 College Street, in Battle Creek; she is buried in Oak Hill Cemetery, next to her grandson Sammy Banks.

Chapter 1

WAY DOWN IN
EGYPT'S LAND

It was around the year 1797. The nation was still in its infancy, this new experiment in democracy called the United States of America. Its first president, the celebrated General George Washington, was receiving a fond farewell from a grateful citizenry as he prepared to complete his second and last term of office. But the excited hopefulness of this new birth was clouded by a lingering problem, one might say a "birth defect": the legal practice of slavery, through which human beings were bought and sold in the marketplace, like the livestock and farm equipment that were put in service to bring prosperity out of the nation's fertile soil and rich natural resources. Imported Africans were bound to a lifetime of unpaid, hard labor, without the rights of citizenship, without the freedoms and protections enjoyed by most other inhabitants of the land. This practice of chattel slavery, this "peculiar institution," as some called it, seemed like a *falsehood* in the midst of the noble ideals and principles of the Declaration of Independence and the federal Constitution, through which the nation had been born. Perhaps it was fitting, then, that this time would also see the birth of Truth, that is, Sojourner Truth, born in the midst of slavery but destined to be a clarion voice of challenge to this blemish on the national character.

Her parents were Elizabeth, called Betsey, and James. Both were pure Africans, her mother thought to have been from the Guinea Coast. Betsey was nicknamed Mau-mau Bett—perhaps a respectful prefacing of her abbreviated name with a phonetic version of "Mama." Her husband's original name was Makewe, but he came to be called James, for it was common for owners to replace African names with European names. And while neither African tradition nor the practices of slavery called for a second, family name, some of the enslaved took on the name of their owners or another name of their choosing. James acquired the second name "Bomefree" (also spelled "Baumfree"), the Low Dutch word for "tree," because his physique was tall and straight, like a tree. This family was the property of one Colonel Johannes Hardenbergh, a wealthy Dutch farmer of Hurley village, Ulster County, in what is now the state of New York. Hardenbergh served on the New York colonial assembly and was a commander in the Continental Army in the American Revolutionary War. In those days this hilly region, inhabited by Mohawk Indians, had been settled by immigrants from the Netherlands. They lived a lifestyle much like they had known in the old country and placed on their new home the stamp of Dutch culture, giving towns, rivers, and other landscape features names from the old country. For instance, Hurley originally bore the Dutch name Nieuw Dorp; present-day New York City was called Nieuw Amsterdam.

The second youngest of 12 or 13 children born to Betsey and James Bomefree was a girl, who was given the name Isabella. "Belle," as her parents called her, might have experienced the joys and challenges of being the "baby" in a large family, but she never had the opportunity, for all of her older siblings had been sold away before she was old enough to know them. How perplexing and painful it must have been for her young mind to witness so often the ceaseless mourning of her parents for the children snatched away by a system that claimed to believe that the natural bonds of parental love did not exist in the hearts of the enslaved. How did she and her younger brother Peter deal with the story, regularly recounted by Mau-mau Bett and James, in words alternating with tears, of a brother who awoke one morning, dutifully prepared the cookstove for his mother, and called her to see his accomplishment, but was interrupted by a sight of delight: a horse-drawn sleigh parking at the door of the owner's house. Confused by the act of drivers of that sleigh thrusting him into the vehicle, without apparent reason, and horrified to see his sister brought out and locked in the sleigh box, the boy ran into the house and hid under a bed, from which the strange men quickly retrieved him, returned him to the sleigh, and drove off, affording his grief-stricken parents the last image they would have of these children of their loins. These were the kinds of family stories into which Belle was born, stories imprinted on her mind, stories she would eventually dedicate her life to rewriting. But for now, they became part of her own daily drama.

Belle's original owner, Johannes Hardenbergh, died in 1799, so she and her family, along with the other property of their owner, were inherited by his son Charles. This had its benefits, because Charles rewarded James and Mau-mau Bett's hardworking, submissive service by promising them a plot of land which they could farm, trading its produce for additional food and material goods to improve the family's lot. But Charles wanted to improve his own living situation, so he built a new residence, complete with space to be used as a hotel. The cellar underneath the new place, however, with its plank and dirt floor, and the absence of any privacy walls or provisions for heating, ventilation, or light, except for a few small windows, was to be the living quarters for all of his enslaved workers—male, female, single, and families, including the Bomefree family. This damp, dark space was to be their home, whether in the sweltering heat of summer or the frigid cold of winter. Actually, it was common among the Dutch in this region to lodge their human property in either the inhospitable cellars or the attics of their homes. Such degrading conditions, added to the denigration of slavery itself, could crush the human spirit. And perhaps this happened for some on the Hardenbergh place. But Belle's parents had a resource that sustained their spirits, even as their bodies were worn down. Belle never forgot the times that Mau-mau Bett would call her and her brother Peter together under the stars at night and instruct them in what had been the resource for her survival. Belle recalled the interchange, led off by Mau-mau Bett, in this way:

"My children, there is a God, who hears and sees you."
"A God, Mau-mau? Where does he live?"

"He lives in the sky. And when you are beaten, or cruelly treated, or fall into trouble, you must ask help of Him, and he will always hear and help you."[1]

These words of hope and help stuck with Belle throughout her life; she drew upon them many times when at the end of her human resources.

By the time Belle was about age 11, Charles Hardenbergh followed his father in death, and his property, including the members of Belle's family, was auctioned off to the highest bidder. James Bomefree, who had been the strong and hardy "tree," was by now broken down in body and basically unable to do much productive work anymore. So he was of no sale value. But neither of the Hardenbergh heirs wanted to take responsibility for him, or contribute financially to his care. So they decided to set both him and his wife free, in order that she could look after him and work to earn their upkeep. In so doing, the Hardenberghs were participating in a practice also common among the Dutch, as well as the owners of the enslaved in the South: emancipating older, "used up" workers as a means of avoiding the expense and burden of caring for them as they became infirm and disabled.

The story of Belle and Peter went differently, though; they were sold, each to a separate owner. Belle was sold for $100, in a deal that included a flock of sheep, to a Mr. John Neely, of Kingston, Ulster County. It was the beginning of Belle's personal horror. For while Mr. Neely could understand spoken Dutch, Belle's only language, his wife could not, and she had no patience for the breaks in communication between herself and her new servant. A misinterpreted command, or an assignment not fulfilled to her satisfaction, would provoke Mrs. Neely to extreme anger and likely result in a whipping for Belle. The pains of frequent whippings were intensified by the terror of not knowing when they might come, or why—or even if there needed to be a "why." Of the many such abuses that haunted her memory throughout her life, Belle recounted this example:

One Sunday Morning she was told to go to the barn. On going there, she found her master with a bundle of rods, prepared in the embers, and bound together with cords. When he had tied

her hands together before her, he gave her the most cruel whipping she was ever tortured with. He whipped her till the flesh was
deeply lacerated, and the blood streamed from her wounds—and
the scars remain until the present day to testify to the fact.[2]

On these occasions, she did not forget the counsel of Mau-mau Bett
to pray to God for help. But believing prayers had to be spoken out
loud, as trouble approached, she typically found herself at the disad-
vantage of being in the midst of trouble without forewarning, as in
that Sunday whipping. But her faith in her mother's counsel did not
waver, and she found times when, in fact, it seemed to work just as she
had been taught. One such time involved her release from her abusive
enslavement to the Neely household. Long and hard had she appealed
to her mother's God for that release, as she had also prayed fervently for
a visit from her father. And the promised power of prayer appeared to
receive a double confirmation. For one day, to her great joy, her father
unexpectedly appeared at the Neely home. During his brief visit, she
pleaded with him to help her get to a new situation. Belle was probably
drawing on the knowledge that the enslaved paid attention to which
owners were relatively more lenient than others, and they used whatever persuasive influence they had to get their friends either sold to or
hired out to these "better" owners. Before the year was out, a fisherman
who had somehow come into contact with James Bomefree came to
the Neely home, at Bomefree's urging, to seek the purchase of Belle.
The deal was struck and Belle went to live with a new master, still in
Ulster County, only a few miles away by land, but a far distant place of
experience from what she had known in her horrific, brutal years with
the Neelys.

The new owners, the Martinus Schryver family, opened a different
world of servitude to Belle. While they owned a large farm, they didn't
cultivate it. Instead, their energies went to Mr. Schryver's fishing trade
and to the tavern that this husband and wife operated. Belle was put to
work on chores supporting those livelihoods. The mother who taught
her to pray the Lord's Prayer and to call on God in distress probably
would have been distressed to witness her daughter pulled down in
moral character through her regular interaction with the Schryvers and
the crude and profane crowd that frequented their tavern. But that

downward slide was interrupted when, in 1810, Belle was sold again, this time to John J. Dumont, of New Paltz, still in Ulster County, the last and longest venue of her enslavement.

DEATH OF JAMES AND MAU-MAU BETT BOMEFREE

Father James Bomefree apparently was still active around the time of Belle's transition from the Neely farm to the Schryver household, for he had been instrumental in bringing it about. But sometime thereafter, both he and his beloved wife passed from this life. Allowed to continue to live in the cellar of the Hardenbergh residence, the two of them had managed to scrape by adequately for a time following their release from bondage. After some few years, though, Bett's health began to decline, leading to, among other conditions, some form of palsy. Coming in for dinner on one autumn day, James discovered his wife collapsed on their cellar home floor. Within hours, she was dead. James, now nearly blind and virtually helpless in his crippled state, was left destitute and alone, devastated with grief over the fate that heretofore neither time nor the harsh, unfeeling workings of the slavery system had managed to bring about, the separation from his life's companion, Betsey.

Belle and Peter were allowed a brief visit to honor their mother's remains and to console their father, an undertaking for which none of their efforts seemed adequate, or perhaps could be. They left their father wailing in anguish over both his loss and his own future fate. James struggled on for the next several years, shuttling from one Hardenbergh household to another. The family felt some pity for one who had submissively given himself in unbending service to them for so many decades, so they decided to take turns lodging him. On one of the rare visits she was permitted to make to her father, Belle even offered him what seemed to her a bright prospect: the State of New York had passed legislation that by 1827 slavery would be abolished in the state; she would then reunite with him and devote herself to his care. But James took little hope or comfort in this promise so far off; he was convinced that the arm of his life could not reach it. And then the Hardenberghs, no longer willing to be burdened with caring for James, emancipated another elderly couple and gave them a decrepit cabin for their use, on the condition that they take care of James. But soon both

The east elevation of the Johannes Hardenbergh house
in Ulster County, New York, photographed in the
1930s. Isabella Bomefree was born on the Hardenbergh estate in about 1797. The house was documented by the Works Progress Administration as part
of its Historic American Buildings Survey. Library of
Congress Prints & Photographs Division/HABS NY,
56-KER, 1-2.

husband and wife died, leaving James alone and destitute again. It was
not long before the inevitable overtook him. He died in that isolated
cabin, of hunger and exposure. This faithful servant, having now given
his all, was thought by the Hardenberghs to merit a "good" funeral,
which, as it turns out, consisted of some black paint for his casket and
a jug of alcoholic beverage for the repast.

THE DUMONT YEARS

Purchase by Dumont was a mixed blessing (if one can ever see *blessing* in the status of enslavement). Belle was beginning to gain a grasp
of English, though still communicating in it with difficulty. But while

language was not the issue, Mrs. Dumont presented a face of harsh impatience to Belle, similar to her treatment by Mrs. Neely, while Mr. Dumont was noticeably more tolerant. Mrs. Dumont seemed disposed to see all of Belle's work as inadequate, while Mr. Dumont saw her industriousness, which he praised both to his wife and to his friends. Mrs. Dumont was hostile and scolding, while Mr. Dumont, in the words of one biographer, "was a man of kind feelings [who treated Belle and all] his slaves with the consideration he did his *other* animals, and *more*, perhaps."[3] While Belle regarded her owner in a relatively positive light, compared to others she had known and known of, this reference to her treatment in comparison to that of the *other animals* is illuminated by Belle's response to a question put to her as to whether Dumont ever whipped her. She said, "Oh yes, he sometimes whipped me soundly, though never cruelly. And the most severe whipping he ever give me was because *I* was cruel to a cat."[4]

The tension between Mr. and Mrs. Dumont around their assessment of Belle's service was aggravated by the apparent jealousy, or at least hostility, of one of their hired white servant girls, who seemed to have it in for Belle. Belle recalled the incident in which the potatoes she was assigned to cook for each morning's breakfast mysteriously began to take on a dirty, dingy appearance. Her mistress offered this to Mr. Dumont as one more proof of Belle's poor performance. Each morning, the same thing occurred, until even Mr. Dumont began to turn against Belle. But fortunately for her, Gertrude Dumont, the 10-year-old daughter in the family, had taken fondly to Belle and decided to help her out of this dilemma. Asking Belle to waken her early the next morning, Gertrude offered to tend to the boiling potatoes while Belle went to do her milking. Sure enough, while Belle was away, Kate, the white hired servant, came into the kitchen and furtively dumped a measure of ashes into the potato pot, unaware that Gertrude was watching and marking her actions. When she left, Gertrude went immediately to her parents and reported what had happened. Kate did not deny Gertrude's account. The mystery was now solved, and Belle was exonerated.

What resulted from this situation demonstrates something of the complexity of the thought patterns and behaviors of the permanently enslaved. For some, the endless, unrewarded drudgery, accented by denigrating acts of domination intended to erase from them any initiative of self-affirmation or self-assertion, created a mindset of despair and despondency. For others there was a survival response of counter-insurgency, of doing only the minimum required to fulfill obligations and avoid verbal and physical reprimand, or of aggressively sabotaging the system. For still others, there was an ironic accommodation to the fixed reality of bondage that led them to strive to live up to slavery's expectations, to outwardly embrace its rules, its values, and even its relationships, so as to maximize its minimal rewards and minimize its maximal potential cruelties. In a curious way, often incomprehensible to those not caught in slavery's web, such persons have seemed to have "bought in to the system," to have been psychoemotionally co-opted, to have "gone over to the other side." Thus, for instance, James and Mau-mau Bett Bomefree taught their children always to work hard, never to lie, never to steal—behavioral values at the heart of slavery's interests and contrary to the survival interests of the enslaved, if "slav-ishly" followed. Furthermore, the social values and, sometimes, reli-gious values imparted to the enslaved, as to Belle by her parents, could cause them to maintain accepting, even affectional relationships with their oppressors, to seek from them personal affirmation and approval, even in the face of abusive treatment.

This was the case with Belle. The acquiescence of Mrs. Dumont to Belle's innocence in the potato incident, and Mr. Dumont's positive reinstated praise of her, energized her desire to please him. She worked harder than ever, going beyond her owners' expectations and demands, sometimes foregoing her own physical needs, to be the servant about which he boasted to his friends that though a woman, her capacity for work made her far more valuable to him than he would expect of a man. And while her cohorts in slavery criticized her for acting as "the white folks' nigger," she was unfazed.[5] Perhaps Belle was also acting out of another syndrome sometimes in the minds of the enslaved: the confusion of the oppressor's powers with those of the divine. After all, their owners exercised ultimate power over the lives and fates of the enslaved. Often with support of the clergy, owners represented them-selves as the earthly superintendents of the enslaved on God's behalf and with God's authorization. Even the catechisms and sermons used by some clergy to instruct the enslaved in the tenets of the Christian faith typically asserted that obedience to masters was grounded in the

scriptures and commanded by God. And Belle's own parents had taught
her to be faithful to her master and always thoroughly honest. Thus
Belle remembered from those days of bondage that

> "at this time, she looked upon her master as a *God*; and believed
> that he knew of and could see her at all times, even as God him-
> self. And she used sometimes to confess her delinquencies, from
> the conviction that he already knew them, and that she would
> fare better if she confessed them voluntarily: and if anyone talked
> to her of the injustice of being a slave, she answered them with
> contempt, and immediately told her master. She then firmly be-
> lieved that slavery was right and honorable." And to be a faithful,
> honest servant, she says, "made me true to my God."[6]

And here one sees another factor that has been prevalent in many societies over the ages, whether among the elite or the oppressed, namely,
the concept that the way things are, the given social order, is the divinely sanctioned way—the way things ought to be and not to be challenged.

Belle's efforts to please her owner, Mr. Dumont, did result in his great
approval and his granting to her small prerogatives and favors. But it
could not protect her from a broken heart or from the ways of slavery
that ignored the deep desires of the heart to choose its own loves. In the
Dutch settlement areas of present-day New York and New Jersey, there
was an annual spring festival known as Pinkster. The Dutch word for
Pentecost, Pinkster was an Old World Dutch version of the celebration
of that Christian observance, involving special church attendance, as
well as gatherings of family and friends for a week of music, feasting,
dancing, and general merriment. It was at one such festival that Belle
had chanced to meet a young man named Robert, who was enslaved
on the nearby Catlin family farm. Their friendship grew to romance,
and Robert sought every opportunity to spend time with Belle. But
for Mr. Catlin this was a problem, because if this relationship resulted
in the birth of children, they would become the property of Dumont,
the mother's owner, according to the customs of the times. Catlin had
no intention losing this chance to increase his own property. So he
forbade Robert to visit Belle and instructed him to find a mate on the

Catlin farm. Slavery's rules and the rules of the heart were thus placed in conflict, and Robert chose to follow the latter, secretly visiting Belle whenever opportunity allowed. On one such occasion, though, when Robert stole over to the Dumont's on the mistaken news that Belle was ill, his owner noticed his absence and came searching for him. Upon discovering him, Catlin and the son that accompanied him set in to beating Robert fiercely with canes, until blood drenched his body, all before Belle's horrified gaze. Dumont, however, intervened, protesting to Catlin that no such potentially fatal brutality was going to be permitted on his land. Honoring this objection, Catlin and his son bound Robert with ropes and led him away. Dumont followed them all the way to the Catlin home, to assure himself that Robert's beating would not resume once the Catlins were out of sight. Catlin had accomplished his purpose, though; the relationship that had flowered between Belle and Robert had been crushed under slavery's heel, for she was never to see Robert again. Robert conceded to the power of the system that bound him and took a mate from the Catlin property, though he died a few short years later.

With one love denied, Belle was soon to have another one contrived. In 1815, when Belle was about 18, firmly in the child-bearing age, Dumont followed the economic logic of slavery, as Catlin had done, and pursued the increase of his property holdings by breeding his servant Belle. Increasing one's human property could be done either by the cost method of purchase in the marketplace or the "free" method of breeding amongst one's existing stock. So Dumont chose for Belle a mate from among his lot, Thomas, a man many years Belle's senior. Thomas had been given two former mates, though each had been sold away to other owners. Belle and Thomas had no previous affection for each other, that, of course, not being a consideration of concern to their owner. Belle insisted that they should be married by an actual minister, rather than "jumping the broom," the ceremony some of the enslaved were given, or the direction just to go forth and live together in unofficial marriage. Assenting to the appeal of his loyal servant, Dumont secured the services of an enslaved black minister, and the union was sealed. Despite the arbitrary nature of this coupling, the relationship between Belle and Thomas became congenial enough. They established a household, ultimately bearing five children, four girls and one boy: Diana, Peter, Elizabeth, Sophia, and another child who may have died in infancy.

During her 16 years on the Dumont estate, Belle continued to exhibit her commitment to hard work and loyalty to her owner, whether in domestic duties or labor in the fields. That very fact proved to be the catalyst for a turning point in her life.

"I WILL NOT BE DENIED": WALKING
INTO FREEDOM'S LIGHT

The Dutch settlers in present-day New York State had been avid defenders of slavery. They insisted that it was essential for the viability and prosperity of their colonial enterprise. As early as 1626 they had imported 11 black indentured servants from the West Indies to help in the building of Fort New Amsterdam. While some imported laborers were allowed to gain their freedom, many others were bound to a lifetime of servitude. When the English successfully challenged the Dutch for control of the region, slavery took on a much-expanded presence. The city of New Amsterdam, now called New York, became a thriving center of the slave trade, and by 1720 it counted 4,000 enslaved Africans among its 31,000 residents.

There were, however, vigorous antislavery voices emerging, especially among members of the Society of Friends, the Quakers. They agitated for abolition of the hateful system of human bondage, with its disgraceful, abusive practices. Following the Revolutionary War, there were efforts to have slavery constitutionally banned in the new nation, but these efforts were rebuffed by proslavery forces, who argued that the matter was for the individual states to decide. So some abolitionists, including those in New York, shifted the contest to the state arena. After some small victories, New York finally legislated in 1799 that all enslaved persons in the state born after July 4, 1799, would gradually be freed—women at age 25 and men at age 28. Subsequent legislation, in 1817, decreed that by July 4, 1827, emancipation was to be accomplished for all the enslaved born *before* 1799. Though not certain of her exact birth year, Belle now had a date certain for her freedom.

Belle Bomefree's service to Dumont had been exemplary, and he had never been hesitant to say so. He had rewarded her, as far as slavery and a slaveholder's benevolence typically allowed, by little kindnesses and considerations, as in the instance when he scolded even his own wife for not tending to Belle's crying infant, whom Belle could not comfort without leaving a task to which she had been assigned. Because of his appreciation for all that she had contributed to his fortunes, Dumont approached Belle one day and pledged to her that "if she would do well," continuing her high level of faithful, industrious service to him, he would grant her and Thomas their freedom papers a full year ahead of the legally specified date for emancipation. He would even give them a log cabin on the property as their dwelling.

Belle received this promise with the joyful enthusiasm that one might expect over such a prospect, and she set herself energetically to "doing well." Ironically, in her eager exertions in doing her work, she accidentally injured very badly one of her hands. But, being driven to meet the terms set for her freedom, she declined to slow down or to take the time to attend properly to her wound, and the condition worsened to the point of diminishing her capacity for the very labor she sought to produce, though she never diminished the time and effort put into her assigned tasks. So when July 4, 1826, arrived, the date of her promised emancipation, she went to Dumont to claim her pass to freedom. Dumont, however, reneged. He charged that, due to her crippled hand, she had not lived up to her end of the bargain. Admitting that she had not produced as much as she formerly had been able to do, she said that, nonetheless, she had been steady and faithful and had done a great deal. But Dumont would not hear it. Perhaps he had seen what he judged to be a significant drop in Belle's output, or maybe he had second thoughts about the loss in his farm's productivity in the coming year that Belle's leaving would mean, especially a concern since he was already experiencing some economic setbacks. But for whatever reason, he stood firm in his decision to hold Belle through the final year of legal slavery.

Belle, just as firmly, though, decided that the all-too-familiar practice of owners promising favors in exchange for service, then backing out on their word, was not going to hold her in its deceptive clutch. She would work until she had finished the main task remaining, namely, spinning Dumont's hundred pounds of wool, then she would take what she had earned in a fair deal, her early freedom. Fairness and honest dealing were values implanted in her by her parents, and even if Dumont would not live by principle, she would not stoop to his level—as difficult as it may seem for contemporary observers of this behavior to affirm Belle's version of living with integrity in a system known not to honor integrity. She was committed to do right by Dumont, even if he would not do right by her. This was not the last time this mode of commitment would express itself in her life.

Yet, how could she get away when the time came? She knew of a case of an enslaved man who had been killed for insisting to claim what his owner had promised. While she did not so much fear this from Dumont, she knew she could not just leave in open daylight, since Dumont would simply restrain her. But she was afraid of the dark. So she remembered, again, her mother's advice and called on her God for help. The answer she believed she received was in the form of a plan to leave just before daybreak, as the darkness began to give way to morning, but before the Dumont household awakened. This would give her time to put some distance behind her as she struck toward a hoped-for place of refuge. Thomas, her husband, tried to dissuade Belle from leaving. He, himself, had once run away but was found in New York City and brought back. Now, he thought differently. In less than a year they would all be free anyway, he argued, without the complications and repercussions that attempted escape would surely bring. And what about the children? Belle's mind was not to be changed. Thomas could look after the children, since she would have no foreseeable means to provide for them. Dumont was wrong to break his word, to ignore the value of all she had done for him, to dismiss her case without apparent remorse or sympathy. She saw clearly now, as never so plainly to her before, the blatant injustice of slavery and its exercise of unbridled power over the lives of human beings. She had long since jettisoned the idea of Dumont as a god figure with ultimate prescience and power. But now, his full, raw humanity was boldly displayed, and she had no intention of conceding to him the prerogative to violate her right to fair treatment. She would not be denied her freedom as promised. So, early one fall morning, after she had completed what she determined to be her final obligation to Dumont, Belle tied into a large white cloth a few belongings and food for the journey, gathered up her infant daughter Sophia, and struck out on her walk to freedom.

NOTES

1. Samuel Sillen, *Women Against Slavery* (New York: Masses & Mainstream, 1955), pp. 17–18.

2. Ibid., pp. 26–27.

3. Ibid., p. 30.

4. Ibid., p. 33.

5. Olive Gilbert, *Narrative of Sojourner Truth, a Northern Slave* (Boston: J. B. Yerrington and Son, Printers, 1850), pp. 31–33.

6. Ibid., pp. 33–34.

Chapter 2

THROUGH MANY DANGERS, TOILS, AND SNARES

As the rising sun dismissed into the past the nighttime of her bondage, Belle surveyed the surrounding scene for evidence of pursuing captors. Had Dumont chanced to an early awakening and found her gone? Would her exodus be so soon thwarted and reversed? But seeing no one, she paused to feed her infant cotraveler and continued to . . . where? That part had not yet been figured out—actually not even thought about! Where *was* freedom? She had not a clue. But she recalled, again, that there was One whose benevolent care could provide for her the solution to her quandary. Praying for help, it shortly came to her that down the same road on which she was already traveling was a man, Levi Rowe, who surely would give her aid. Making her way to his house, she found him both welcoming and helpful, as he pointed her to two households that likely could provide the safe harbor she was seeking. At the first of these two places, Isaac and Maria Van Wagenen, a kindly, religious couple, sympathized with her case and agreed to take her in and give her work to earn her keep. As night fell, there ended this first scene in the unfolding drama of Belle's self-actualization.

An appearance at the Van Wagenen's porch the next morning, though, brought Belle no surprise. It was Dumont, whom she had expected would be fast behind her. She had not intended to hide or to give him a hard time in finding her, which showed an amazing degree of considerateness on her part. This was also a window into her character of deeply genuine human compassion, the capacity to care about even her enemies, as her faith taught. This capacity would undergird the way in which she would pursue the journey for universal justice, a vocation beyond the horizon of her conscious intentions at this time.

To Dumont's chiding that she had run away from him, she retorted that she had *walked*, not run. To his insistence that she return with him, she was clear with him that that was not an option. To his threat that he would therefore seize her child, she let him know, in no uncertain terms, that she was definitely not going to allow that to happen.

At this point, the generosity of Mr. Van Wagenen provided the resolution to this mounting confrontation; he would *buy out* Belle's remaining time of service to Dumont. Receiving his stated price of $20 for Belle, plus $5 for the child, Dumont turned and left. Belle's audacious plan to sever her connection to the duplicitous Dumont had succeeded, and now she had a new master, who seemed by all appearances to be the type one could only dream to have. But a new *master?* Not so, said Van Wagenen. He was quick to correct any such thought Belle might be entertaining. First, he said he opposed the practice of slavery itself, and its buying and selling of human beings. He dealt with Dumont only as the lesser evil to avoid her being dragged back to her degraded former life. But more important, even though his purchase made her technically his possession, he wanted Belle clearly to know that "There is but one master, and he who is *your* master is *my* master." What, then, should she call her new legal owners? "Call me Isaac Van Wagenen, and my wife is Maria Van Wagenen." And from that day, she called herself Isabella Van Wagenen.[1]

"I'LL HAVE MY CHILD AGAIN"

In taking her leave of Dumont, Isabella had brought with her her recently born infant child, Sophia, but had left behind her husband and two of her other children. Some commentators on Isabella's life have suggested that the arbitrary, imposed nature of her marriage to

Thomas, along with the dehumanizing nature of slavery itself, muted any genuine sense of family connectedness or true affection for husband and children. In relation to Thomas, perhaps there was at least a kernel of truth to this notion. Having been denied her romance with Robert, then joined to Thomas for breeding purposes, in a ceremony that, as in all unions between the enslaved, was neither legally binding nor permanent, it would not be surprising if bonds of affection did not develop. And, in fact, two of the Dumont children in later years recollected that there had been tensions in Isabella and Thomas's relationship. But whatever the character of Isabella's sense of connection to Thomas, the subsequent narrative of her life gives no evidence that she was not bonded to her children, or to others in her parental family, even to siblings she had never known.

A very striking case in point, one that was a preview of the mark Isabella was to make on history, was that of her son Peter. He had been named after her younger brother, who, along with her, had been sold away from their parents, each to a different buyer, after the death of their owner Charles Hardenbergh. As the rules of slavery allowed, Isabella's Peter, age five, was sold away from her shortly before her break with Dumont. He was bought by a dentist by the name of Dr. Gidney, who was soon returning to England and who thought Peter would make a fine personal servant. But later rethinking his decision, he turned Peter over to his brother, Solomon Gidney, a neighbor to the Dumonts. Solomon Gidney then sold Peter to his wife's brother, a Mr. Fowler, who took Peter to slavery in Alabama.

Months later, when Isabella learned that Peter had been sold into southern slavery, she was impelled to action by fear for the fate of her son and by anger at this illegal transaction. She learned from friends that New York law prohibited selling or transporting enslaved persons out of the state, as a precaution against those who would do so to avoid having to free them by the stipulated 1827 general emancipation date. First she approached the Dumonts, who had started the process by selling Peter. Mrs. Dumont dismissed Isabella's complaints with this telling response, recalled by Isabella in her *Narrative*:

> Ugh! A fine mess to make about a little *nigger*! Why, haven't you
> as many of 'em left as you can see to, and take care of? A pity 'tis,

the niggers are not all in Guinea!! Making such a halloo-balloo about the neighborhood; and all for a paltry nigger!!![2]

But the chilling effect Mrs. Dumont intended the words to accomplish instead was answered by Isabella's cool, steely reply: "I'll have my child again!" How possibly could that be, Mrs. Dumont cynically questioned. "Have your child again! How can you get him? And what have you to support him with, if you could? Have you any money?"

Calmly Isabella answered the taunt: "No. I have no money, but God has enough, or what's better! And I'll have my child again." Looking back on that day, Isabella recaptured the rush of confident, faith-based courage that surrounded the moment, saying, "Oh my God! I know'd I'd have him again. I was sure God would help me to get him. Why, I felt so *tall* within—I felt as if the *power of a nation* was with me!"

The sensation of empowerment generated in her encounter with the callous Mrs. Dumont carried over to her confrontation with the Gidneys, to whom she next went. Finding not Solomon Gidney, but his mother-in-law, she poured out of her heart the grief mingled with fear in which the sale of Peter had enveloped her, perhaps believing that mother to mother some sympathy might be found, and some comradeship in reversing Peter's situation. Instead, the elder Mrs. Gidney mocked Isabella's plaintive concern and asked if Isabella thought her child was better than her own child, the new Mrs. Fowler, who also had gone off to Alabama. Would not the life of plenty and kindly treatment living with her daughter be better than what Peter left behind? But Isabella called out Mrs. Gidney on this false comparison between the prospects of a married, free white woman and a vulnerable, enslaved child. Still, Mrs. Gidney could only muster a mad, maniacal laughter of derision at an anguished mother. Isabella, though, believed firmly that since help was not forthcoming there, she had another source of greater capacity to help. She called on her God to demonstrate that it was so. And she believed that, before long, God did.

Sometime soon after this event, Isabella met a man, whose identity her *Narrative* holds in anonymity, who told her that there were Quakers in the nearby Poppletown neighborhood that might be able to help her in her quest to reclaim her son. The Quakers were known for their antislavery position. They were the first religious group in the nation to take a public stance against slavery and to disallow it among their members. The man pointed out to her two particular houses where she might find such sympathizers, and she went immediately to them and told her story. As it turns out, they had already heard of what had happened to her and were ready to assist in such ways as they could. Giving her lodging for the night, the next morning they arranged for her to be taken to the town of Kingston and instructed her to go before the grand jury at the courthouse there and enter a formal complaint.

A couple of amusing incidents followed that reflected the innocence of one with no previous opportunity to learn the ways of the public world. First, responding to the instruction to speak to the grand jury, Isabella addressed the first man she saw that looked to her to be "grand" and began telling him her purpose. Hearing her complaint, he bemusedly escorted her to the room where sat the actual grand jurors. They in turn asked her if she was willing to swear that the child in question was her son, and when she agreed to do so, they handed her a Bible to swear by. Isabella put the book to her lips and began speaking into it. After a period of laughter by the group present, an attorney, Esquire Chip, instructed her in the proper procedure, and the oath was taken. She was given a writ that was to be served on Solomon Gidney by the constable at New Paltz.

In the face of the unfolding legal events, Gidney was advised by his lawyer that he had better retrieve Peter from Alabama, lest he be found guilty in the case and face a heavy fine and imprisonment. By the next spring, Gidney returned with the boy, although he did not turn him over to Isabella, which had been her hope. She feared that while in Gidney's custody, Peter would be abused to spite her for the lawsuit, especially if it was successful.

The next opportunity for Isabella's case to come up on the court docket was several months away. But she was too impatient to wait that long. Her prayer had been for the immediate deliverance of her son, and she was determined to have that outcome, though she feared that God might be getting tired of her pressing, as the attorneys apparently had. Yet it was a perfect stranger who came up to her and provided the doorway into the answer to her prayer. He told her that down the road lived lawyer Demain, who surely could do for her what she wanted. Going straightway to Demain's place, she laid her case out and sought his help. Demain confidently informed her that if she could come up with five dollars, he would have her son released to her in 24 hours. Objecting that she had no five dollars, nor had ever had even a dollar, Demain insisted both on his fee and on the certainty of his success in gaining back her son. Go to the Quakers in Poppletown, he said; you can raise the funds from them. She went; and she did. She raised more than the required five dollars but gave it all to Demain, though others said she should have kept the overage and used it to buy herself some shoes, she being without any at the time. But her reply was that it was her son she wanted, not clothes, and "If five dollars will get him, more will *surely* get him."

By evening of the next day, Demain had fulfilled his commitment; Peter had been delivered to the place where Demain had told Isabella to meet him. Gidney was there, as was the judge of the court. What followed, though, Isabella could not have anticipated, nor would she have wanted to believe. Upon seeing her, Peter recoiled in fear. In intense tears, he begged to be allowed to remain with Gidney and not be given to the woman who he said was falsely claiming to be his mother. When questioned by the court about the scarring on his face and body, Peter, nervously looking at Gidney, explained them as the result of accidents. The justice apparently was not persuaded by Peter's words. And when all testimony had been heard and cases made by legal counsel, the judge decreed that Peter was to be turned over to Isabella, his mother, though Peter was still wailing and pleading that it not be done.

Peter had probably been led by Fowler, his new owner, to believe that his mother was a monstrous person that he should fear. And when Isabella and Demain managed to calm Peter down and convince him that he could speak truthfully without repercussions from Gidney, he revealed that the scars and healed-over wounds that covered his body resulted from brutal punishments administered by Fowler—being "whipped, kicked, and beat." He said Fowler's wife, Eliza, had regretted his ever having been brought south and had secretly tended to his wounds. The sight of her brutalized son pushed Isabella to an uncharacteristic desire for divine vengeance.

Some months later, while visiting in the home of friends of her former owner, Dumont, Isabella overheard the news that Mr. Fowler had beaten his wife Eliza to death in a gruesome fit of passion. Isabella's sense of pity for Eliza Fowler and her now orphaned children was moderated by the still fresh pain over what had happened to her own child while in the Fowler household. Still, she remembered in later years, looking back on Eliza Fowler's fate, that "I dared not find fault with God, exactly; but the language of my heart was, 'Oh my God! That's too much—I did not mean quite so much, God!'"

A TRANSFORMING FAITH ENCOUNTER

As this last incident illustrates, by now Isabella had developed a spiritual life that was a significant resource for her in the challenges she faced. It had been planted in her as a child by her parents, especially Mau-mau Bett, who sat her and brother Peter down under the stars and told them of a God in the sky who cared about their troubles and would help and protect them if ever they prayed for it. The confidence of Mau-mau Bett in this belief and her sincerity in living it out were imprinted on young Isabella's own spirit.

Though the culture of her Dutch community included a Christian church component, it is not easy to say that Mau-mau Bett's teachings were Christian, per se. Imported Africans brought with them from their heritage a full-blown religious life, with belief in a supreme Creator God, who was all-wise and all-powerful. This God worked in the world supporting life in every aspect of creation—human, animal, plant, and the larger physical environment. And this God enforced goodness and justice in human relationships. Such an understanding of God and God's activity was present in Christian teachings, too. But owners of the enslaved were hesitant to introduce their human property to their faith. For some owners, such a thing did not seem necessary since, in their minds, their animal property and their human property were just two forms of the same thing, namely, work animals. For those who admitted the full humanity of the enslaved, the problem was that, according to the customs of the times, it was not permissible for a Christian to hold other Christians in slavery. So to convert their human subjects to the faith meant that they would have to set them free. Furthermore, a Christianized African might expect to be treated as an equal, as a brother or sister human, a claim most whites seemed unwilling to honor. And if Christianized and still held in bondage, they might likely see the contradiction between their slave status and their freedom in Christ and rebel against their enslavement. Some own-ers either ignored these various difficulties and followed their sense of Christian duty to bring the faith to all persons under their care, or they combined caution with duty by providing for a form of Christian teach-ing to the enslaved that reinforced the slavery status by claiming divine approval of it. For instance, a common sermon text for preaching to the enslaved was Ephesians 6:5: "Servants, be obedient to them that are your masters according to the flesh, with fear and trembling, in single-ness of your heart, as unto Christ" (from the King James Version). In religious instruction to the enslaved, biblical virtues that aligned with slavery's interests would be emphasized, such as the commandments against stealing, killing, and dishonesty.

There is no direct evidence in Isabella's biographical narrative that either she or her parents attended church services or were given reli-gious instruction. In fact, at one point Isabella says outright that prior to full adulthood she had never been to any church. Yet the religious system she inherited from her parents and that she came to live by does seem to have had an increasingly distinct Christian flavor. Mau-mau Bett's remembered words made no reference to Jesus, nor to the Chris-tian salvation story, but she clearly impressed upon Isabella the bibli-cal virtues she had been taught. Isabella recalled that as a mother she would let her children go hungry, even corporally punish them when they cried out in hunger for food, rather than to steal from her owners to feed them.

As her religious life unfolded through her experiences of enslave-ment under various owners, Isabella had developed a practice of daily prayer, laying all of her issues before God and promising good behavior as her return for God's hoped-for answers to her lists of wants—almost *demands* for God's aid. But she regularly, even daily, failed in keeping her end of the bargain, yielding to temptations to anger and behaviors she knew were not pleasing to God. Some of these ways had been picked up during her stay in the tavern environment with the Schryvers. But she would return to detailed prayer requests the next day, with promises again to be good. Because Isabella's understanding of God was simply as the rescuer from trouble, it was easy to smooth over her bad behavior and natural to disconnect from prayer and lose touch with that God when troubles subsided. Isabella had walked from bondage to the relatively good life in the Van Wagenen household. With all of her wishes essentially now fulfilled, the motivation for prayer faded.

But Isabella's view of God was soon to change, profoundly, and in a way that set the stage for the vocation that also would change her name. The occasion for the life-altering event was another of the same Pinkster festivals in which she had earlier met and fallen into the aborted love relationship with Robert. Isabella was grateful for her good new situation with the Van Wagenens and could not have imagined anything better, but as Pinkster approached, she began to think back nostalgically on this major party time. It was a sharp contrast to her present tame, low-key existence. The pull of the former times of merriment with old friends and family, in fact, led her to what may seem like a strange, contradictory decision—to return to live under the Dumonts. As Pinkster time approached, Isabella had a premonition that Dumont was going to come, unannounced, to the Van Wagenen home. Sure enough, he did. And surely to his surprise, she informed him that she and infant Sophia were going with him when he returned home. As though rejecting this as an insult added to the injury he felt Isabella had dealt him, Dumont refused to consent. But Isabella was determined to go, so she gathered her things and her child and headed for Dumont's carriage. And here, the words from Isabella's *Narrative* must be called upon to convey the character and impact of what happened next:

> But, ere she reached the vehicle, she says that God revealed himself to her, with all the suddenness of a flash of lightning, showing her, "in the twinkling of an eye, that he was *all over*"—that he pervaded the universe—"and that there was no place that God was not." She became instantly conscious of her great sin in forgetting her almighty Friend and "ever-present help in time of trouble." All her unfulfilled promises arose before her, like a vexed sea whose waves run mountains high; and her soul, which seemed but one mass of lies, shrunk back aghast from the "awful look" of him whom she had formerly talked to, as if he had been a being like herself; and she would now fain have hid herself in the bowels of the earth, to have escaped his dread presence. But she

plainly saw that there was no place, not even in hell, where he was not; and where could she flee? Another such "a look," as she expressed it and she felt that she must be extinguished forever, even as one, with the breath of his mouth, "blows out a lamp,' so that no spark remains."

The second "look" that Isabella feared would annihilate her did not come, but the fear of it remained. As important as was this fear was her other response. In simple words she expressed a new insight into the nature of the God she thought she knew: "Oh God, I did not know you were so big." The God who was, in effect, the errand runner for human requests was becoming the cosmic sovereign Mau-mau Bett had tried to reveal to Isabella and Peter, the one who she said inhabited the skies, whose moon and stars looked down upon their slavery-scattered siblings, no matter how far separated from them.

Rescued in the nick of time from her attempt to return to "Egypt," as she named her former bondage, with Dumont now out of sight, but feeling the urgency to speak again to this newly manifest God, Isabella was caught up by a deep sense of unworthiness to do so. She could not brashly step up to God as she had formerly done, as though God were a peer, or just a cut above. She needed someone else to speak on her behalf, someone who was worthy to shield her from the deserved wrath of God. She had a vision of a close friend approaching to fill that role, until it occurred to her that that friend was no more worthy than she herself. Then another vision appeared, of a heavenly-type figure, whom it seemed that at the same time she both knew and did not know. When she pleaded to know who he was, the answer came back, "It is Jesus."

Mau-mau Bett had not spoken to Isabella of Jesus; over the course of her still young years she had heard of him but had no clear idea of who he was, other than a great man of some kind. But in this encounter, he appeared to her as a treasure of loveliness and goodness, possessing the transcendent worthiness to stand before God on her behalf. Most importantly, he would do so, because he *loved her* and, though she had been unaware, he had always loved her. The fear of the breath of God snuffing out her life was now removed by the presence of one who would stand between her and the righteous God and reconcile her to him. The excitement and joy this new relationship brought gave her a new sense of purpose in life and changed the way she saw other people. One of the Negro Spirituals sung by the enslaved says that religion "makes you love everybody." Though Isabella would not likely have heard this song sung in her area, it was, in fact, her testimony. For she recalled in later years that after her dramatic encounter with Jesus, "When the love come in me . . . I said, 'Yea, God, I'll love everybody and the white people, too.'"[3]

Following this life-changing experience of religious conversion, Isabella joined the Methodist church in Kingston. In conversations with members there, she learned that Jesus was not just her secret, personal friend but was known by all Christians and that he was divine. She did not bother herself with the debates about Jesus's divine or human make-up. She was content to rest the matter in her own experience with him and what it meant to her life, that her confidence in him, like her confidence in the power of prayer, would be more than enough to carry her through whatever might lie ahead. The proof positive to her was the outcome of her prayers for God's aid in the recovery of her son, Peter. An impoverished, unlearned, barefoot black woman went up against eminent white men of power and influence. To her mind, "Only God could have made such people hear me; and he did it in answer to my prayers."[4]

NOTES

1. Olive Gilbert, *Narrative of Sojourner Truth, a Northern Slave* (Boston: J. B. Yerrington and Son, Printers, 1850), pp. 43–44.

2. This and subsequent quotes illustrating the saga of Isabella's effort to regain custody of her son Peter are taken from Gilbert, *Narrative*, pp. 45–58.

3. Carleton Mabee, *Sojourner Truth: Slave, Prophet, Legend* (New York: New York University Press, 1993), p. 22.

4. Gilbert, *Narrative*, p. 71.

Chapter 3

IN THE VALLEY
OF THE SHADOW

Shortly after her official emancipation by the State of New York in 1827, Isabella had left the Van Wagenen household and moved to Kingston, where she worked in such domestic employment as she could find. Oddly enough, one of her employers was a Mr. Fred Waring, an uncle to Solomon Gidney, against both of whom she had just done battle in court. This may have been an example of her new "love everybody" ethic, resulting from her conversion. At any rate, after gaining custody of Peter, Isabella made a decision in 1829 to try to better her life in New York City. At a church meeting in Kingston, Isabella had met a Miss Gear, a schoolteacher who was vacationing there from New York. Gear spoke to Isabella of the prospects in the city for one with her good mind and work abilities. Isabella was persuaded to give it a try. Perhaps she, like many others before and after her, believed that the concentration of people and resources that cities represent would offer expanded opportunities for advancement not available in rural towns. What Isabella was to find, as others have also found, is that cities offer a variety of types of opportunities, not all of which turn out to be in one's best interests. But initially, things went well. Miss Gear connected her to a friend who supplied her with domestic employment and lodging for her and Peter. And Isabella affiliated, again, with Methodism, first joining the John Street Methodist Episcopal Church and later moving her membership to a congregation of the African Methodist Episcopal (AME) Zion Church, a recently formed black denomination.

In what might seem to be another oddity, either upon her move to New York or just after it, Isabella took her toddler daughter Sophia to live again with the Dumonts. Presumably the explanation for this was that her children that still remained there could look after Sophia, it not being feasible for Isabella to do so, given the limited accommodations and pay afforded to domestics. Her husband Thomas had been emancipated but was aged and ill; Isabella's daughters were also emancipated, but they were bound by the terms of emancipation to serve their owner until a legally fixed age.

With Sophia now in trusted care, Isabella opened herself to the new experiences of city life, determined, though, not to "bow to the filth of the city."[1] But what Isabella did not anticipate was how city ways would lead to the downward descent of the son she had so valiantly and incredibly managed to rescue from slavery. Peter was a very bright and amiable young fellow. His quick wit and pleasing personality gave promise of a good future for himself, as far as the prospects for young blacks in that day went. But as he grew and formed friendships over the first two or three years, they were among persons who introduced him to the underside of city life, with its negative temptations. And Peter succumbed. While keeping an outward appearance of being the son in which Isabella could take pride—and indeed she did—Peter fell into a life of crime. He even took an alias, going in public as Peter Williams, to cover any trail that might enable the knowledge of his deeds to get back to his mother. But inevitably, it did. Several times he was arrested and jailed for stealing. Isabella would bail him out and he would repent of his wrongdoing and promise to do better, but then he would return to the streets and into trouble again.

With the financial assistance of a friend who believed in Peter's potential, Isabella attempted to arrest this downward spiral by enrolling Peter in a navigation school. But he ditched classes and instead spent his time loitering with friends, though convincing the teacher that he had legitimate excuses for his absences and making it appear to his mother that he was going to class and doing his work. When his deception became known, Isabella and her friend found employment for Peter, but he lost the job due to stealing from his employer. With Peter always pleading his remorse and intention to do right but never managing to stay on the path, Isabella finally grew exasperated and decided to cut the rescue cord, to see if that would teach him the lesson he needed to learn about the consequences of his behavior. Maybe this would turn him around. When arrested again, Peter called for his mother to bail him out, but she refused to come; she left him in jail.

However, the real Mr. Peter Williams, hearing of the incarceration of one claiming his name, went to the jail and, learning from Peter about his mother and their family story, decided to arrange for his release to give him the chance to redeem himself. Peter promised that he would leave New York and the reckless life he had been drawn into, by joining the crew of the whaling vessel *Zone,* of Nantucket, which was due to depart within a week. Jaded by his previous unfulfilled promises to straighten his life out, Isabella heard this latest rendition with disbelief. She expected—maybe even more *feared*—that when that boat weighed anchor in the coming week, it would be without Peter, that he would show up in town with another bogus excuse. Even the report from Mr. Williams that Peter had, indeed, sailed away that August of 1839 did not assure her of his departure, until she received this letter dated October 17, 1840:

My Dear and Beloved Mother:

I take this opportunity to write to you and inform you that I am well, and in hopes for to find you the same. I am got on board the same unlucky ship Zone, of Nantucket. I am sorry for to say, that I have been punished once severely, by shoving my head in the fire for other folks. We have had bad luck, but in hopes to have better. We have about 230 on board, but in hopes, if I don't have good luck, that my parents will receive me with thanks. I would like to know how my sisters are. Does my cousins live in New York yet? Have you got my letter? If not, inquire to Mr. Peirce Whiting's. I wish you would write me an answer as soon as possible. I am your only son, that is so far from your home, in the wide, briny ocean. I have seen more of world than ever I expected, and if I ever should return home safe, I will tell you all my troubles and hardships. Mother, I hope you do not forget me, your dear and only son. I should like to know how Sophia, and Betsey, and Hannah, come on. I hope that you all will forgive me for all that I have done.

Your son,
'PETER VAN WAGENER.'

Over the next year Isabella received two other letters from Peter, the last ending with a tender request and a poem:

Notice—when this you see, remember, and place me in your mind.

Get me to my home, that's in the far-distant west,
To the scenes of my childhood, that I like the best;
There the tall cedars grow, and the bright waters flow,
Where my parents will greet me, white man, let me go!
Let me go to the spot where the cataract plays,
Where oft I have sported in my boyish days;
And there is my poor mother, whose heart ever flows,
At the sight of her poor child, to her let me go, let me go!

'Your only son,
'PETER VAN WAGENER'

This was the last she was ever to hear from or about him. When the *Zone* sailed back into New York harbor in May of 1843, Peter was not on board and there was no word of his whereabouts. Looking back over the years, Isabella recalled the wistful ruminations of a mother's heart at her son's absence: "He is good now, I have no doubt; I feel sure that he has persevered, and kept the resolve he made before he left home;—he seemed so different before he went, so determined to do better."[2]

LOST AND FOUND

If the decision to relocate to New York led to Peter's loss of innocence and Isabella's loss of Peter to an unknown fate, it also set the stage for a serendipity of reunion, a recovery of relationships that none involved ever dreamed would happen. One of Isabella's sisters, Sophia, whom she had not seen for 17 years, had moved to New York City from where she had been living in Newberg, New York. And it was quite probably at the AME Zion church that these two disconnected family members chanced to meet. Though hardly recognizing each other at first, given the changes that time had made on each of them, they at last saw, through the veil of time, faces that once lived in the same moment. More amazing, Sophia told Isabella that their brother Michael was also living in New York, and she took her to meet him. Michael was the one about whom Mau-mau Bett had so longingly, poignantly spoken in her tale of the child carried away in the sleigh that fateful day so long before. What was more, Michael related that another sister, Nancy, who had been locked in the box and exiled with him in that self-same sleigh, had also been living in New York, though she had recently died. What an event for Isabella, to come into the flesh-and-blood presence of siblings whom she had known only through the tortured memories of her parents, and who she had assumed she had lost forever to slavery. And even though Nancy was not there in this Bomefree reunion, Isabella had, in fact, been in her flesh-and-blood presence, for Michael told her that Nancy had been a member of the AME Zion congregation in the city, where Isabella had joined, and as he described Nancy to Isabella, she remembered kneeling at the altar with this woman and shaking her hand in the acts of greeting customary in that Christian community. Tears freely flowed from the three of these children of James and Mau-mau Bett, tears whose deep meanings could only be known by them. These three, in Mau-mau Bett's words, were ones the same stars and same moon had looked down upon, though slavery's arm had pulled them apart, but they were now reunited in the sunlight of freedom.

THE HARVEST IS PLENTIFUL, BUT THE LABORERS ARE SUSPECT

The early 19th century was a time of mounting religious ferment, of many types. Settlers moving ever westward, seeking their fortunes in the frontier regions beyond traditional eastern settlement, saw the emergence of the lively camp meeting and revival phenomena. Frontier people gathered in designated campgrounds from their remote wilderness dwellings for one- and two-week series of intense religious services of preaching, praying, fervent singing, and exhortation to adopt, or renew, a commitment to Christian living. New religious groups were claiming special divine revelations that required of their followers a disciplined, self-sacrificial, nonworldly style of living. Some predicted the catastrophic end of the world, with a limited number of faithful believers to be saved from the destruction and a new age of divine rulership to be established.

In the cities, a "moral reform" movement arose, urging Christians to reach out in mission to the persons and places in the community that had fallen to behaviors the church considered immoral and degraded, such as drinking, gambling, prostitution, and behaviors that led, in turn, to poverty and ill-health. This work had special appeal to women, who saw in it the opportunity to move beyond their socially prescribed domestic sphere of service. The roles designated for women in this time period were based on the assumption that women were naturally gifted to do physically nurturing, caregiving work; instruction of the young; providing the support functions for family well-being; and upholding and advancing the religious and moral foundations of society, beginning with religious nurture in the home. All these functions were to be based in the home; that was "women's sphere." Men's "sphere" was understood to be the public arena, taking leadership in business, defense, and religious and societal governance. But the goal of moral reform of society opened the way for women to take their home-based "gifts" and the related functions and apply them in the community—nurturing, caregiving, educating, and addressing issues of moral and religious deficiency. Thus, they would be doing socially acceptable "women's work," but in a larger arena. And they brought to it a natural, particular concern to do this work *on behalf of women*, the more vulnerable half of the social body.

It was into this atmosphere that Isabella Van Wagenen entered as she left her rural residence for life in the city. Miss Gear, who had accompanied Isabella to New York and found her lodging and employment, also recruited her to work in social moral reform. She and teams of women visited "abodes of vice and misery" and experienced successes in reclaiming wayward lives and in establishing prayer meetings for those drawn in.[3] But something more momentous lay ahead in Isabella's path of growth in religious understanding and service. Once, while attending a prayer meeting, she met a Mr. Elijah Pierson, who later hired her to do live-in domestic service in his home. Pierson was a Baptist layperson who had developed religious beliefs and practices that included fasting, faith healing, a simple lifestyle, and dependence on direct communication with the Spirit of God. He claimed to have received a direct message from God, in these words: "Thou art Elijah, the Tishbite. Gather unto me all the members of Israel at the foot of Mt. Carmel."

Impressed by Pierson's forceful spirituality, Isabella left the AME Zion congregation and joined the small group of Pierson's family and others that Pierson had gathered under his leadership. They called themselves the "Kingdom," in keeping with their goal of establishing the Kingdom of God on earth. Isabella was an active participant in their devotional meetings and adopted the practice of fasting.

Some time after allegedly receiving his message from God, Pierson met Robert Matthews, another who believed himself to be divinely appointed to a special mission of religious leadership. After failing in business in Cambridge, New York, Matthews came to Albany and by 1829 was involved in street preaching. In 1830, he claimed to have received the revelation that the mark of the true Christian man was the refusal to shave. Further, he believed he was given a mission to convert the world. Taking the name Matthias, after the New Testament apostle of Jesus, and calling himself a Jew, he went on an evangelistic mission across the Northeast, eventually coming to New York City. There, in May 1832, he felt led to visit Pierson, whom he had not previously met.

Pierson was not at home when Matthias arrived, so he introduced himself to Isabella. She thought he looked like the Jesus figure in her conversion vision. After an extended conversation, Isabella was taken by what she heard and "felt as if God had sent him to set up the kingdom."[4] Learning from Isabella that Pierson held beliefs similar to his, Matthias indicated that he would return to talk with Pierson personally at another time. When, after a few days, that conversation took place, Isabella was allowed to be present. After sharing their individual beliefs and calls to mission, Pierson and Matthias found themselves to be of a common mind and agreed to collaborate in a common cause. Matthias would hold the position as God on earth, since he possessed

the spirit of God, and Pierson would be his John the Baptist, the pro-
claimer and validator of Matthias's identity. Together, they preached
that they were the sole voices of truth and the only entry way into
the Kingdom, which it was their task to bring about across the earth.
Women were neither to be taught nor to engage in religious leadership, since women were "full of all deviltry." They asserted that neither
prayer nor Holy Communion had any efficacy. Other traditional Christian beliefs were also called into question, and certain dietary restrictions were prescribed for true believers.[5]

Isabella apparently accepted the Matthias/Pierson teachings, in
spite of their subordination of women and denigration of women's status. She accepted employment to do Matthias's washing, even after
hiring on with another domestic employer. Though she had joined
various Methodist congregations and sat under their teaching, she had
balanced what she heard with her own spiritual intuitions, which she
trusted. For instance, when presented with the controversy over the
divine versus human nature of Jesus and the orthodox position that
Jesus was God, she took the position that "Of that I only know as I saw.
I did not see him [in her conversion vision] to be God; else, how could
he stand between me and God? I saw him as a friend, standing between
me and God, through whom, loved flowed as from a fountain."[6] So
hers was a belief system that was open and "under construction" as she
went. Isabella, while enslaved, had never fully challenged the correct-
ness of slavery as an institution, nor the legitimacy of the authority of
her owners. Perhaps her ability to accept the discipline and authoritar-
ian model inherent in the Matthias and Pierson teachings reflected the
lingering presence of this resignation to human systems of authority.

For several years Isabella was active in what came to be called Matthias' Kingdom, even moving to its headquarters in the summer home
and farm of Benjamin H. and Ann Folger, a wealthy New York merchant
family, located near Sing Sing, New York. Though Peter was still in her
care at the time of the move, he does not appear to have come with
her to the Kingdom quarters of the Folgers. She may have placed him
in a residential employment situation during this time. Isabella served
in the Kingdom as a domestic and, according to its practice of members holding all money and property in common, merged her furniture

and savings into the Kingdom's holdings. As a woman, and according to the group's teachings, she could not offer religious leadership, nor offer public prayer. But she participated in all the religious ceremonies and shared in the labor that supported this communal enterprise.

Matthias ruled the Kingdom with an iron hand, while living in high style from its funds. In a move that threatened to disrupt the stability of the Kingdom enterprise, he instituted a policy of joining in marriage persons of "match spirits," including swapping already married persons for those deemed to be their proper match. One such swap involved taking as his "match spirit" Ann Folger, the wife of his benefactor Benjamin Folger, giving to Benjamin, instead, his (Matthias's) own married daughter. Isabella seems to have approved of the general practice of spirit match marriages, though she sympathized with those who suffered from its outcomes, and she, herself, never took part in it.

When Elijah Pierson died at the Kingdom, in August of 1834, from causes related to long-standing bouts with epileptic seizures, suspicions were raised among the civil authorities about the actual cause of death. County officials shut down the Folger House at Sing Sing. Mrs. Folger returned to her husband, and they moved back to their New York home; Isabella and Matthias moved in with them. No longer willing to support the Kingdom, particularly after some financial reverses in the family business, the Folgers encouraged Isabella to move out by offering her $25 and giving Matthias $530, with which he could buy a farm in the West, as he had long wanted to do. In loyalty to Matthias, Isabella gave her money to him, though he returned it to her. He accepted his payment from the Folgers and went to his former home in Albany to prepare for the journey west. Isabella traveled separately, first to visit her children at the Dumont's, then to Albany, in expectation of accompanying Matthias to the West. But a different outcome was in the making. After the departure of Matthias and Isabella from New York, the Folgers contacted the police, charging Matthias with *stealing* the $530 and charging them both with murdering Pierson by poisoning and attempting, likewise, to poison them, the Folgers.

On the strength of character references from former employers, Isabella avoided prosecution. One such reference, a Mr. Whiting, said: "I do state unequivocally that we have never had a servant that did all the work so faithfully, and one in whom we could place such implicit confidence—in fact, we did, and still do, believe her to be a woman of extraordinary moral purity." Matthias, on the other hand, was charged with stealing and with murder. In order to formally clear her name and to be able to stand as a witness in Matthias's defense, she was advised to sue the Folgers for slander. She agreed, reportedly saying, "I have got the truth, and I know it, and I will crush them with the truth." Isabella's slander suit trial resulted in a victory for her and an award of $125, plus costs—a second incredible victory for a black person and a woman, with no formal education, no claim to societal standing, and no resources. What she had was her consistent record of conscientious fulfillment of her commitments, her unshakable courage, her personal integrity, and her dedication to truth.

The courts eventually withdrew the charge of stealing against Matthias, but he was indicted for murder. In his trial, in April of 1835, Isabella was the chief witness for the defense, even though the social custom of the day was to discount or deny, outright, the testimony of black persons. In the absence of substantive medical evidence of poisoning, the jury rendered a verdict of innocence. But the district attorney subsequently brought a charge against Matthias for the incident in which he whipped his married daughter when she initially refused his directive to become Benjamin Folger's "match spirit" wife. Matthias served a four-month sentence upon being convicted of that offense, and then, upon release, departed for the West.

When the Kingdom collapsed, Isabella lost the savings she had placed in its common fund. In the course of the experience, however, she gained some insights into human behavior, some additional reasons to have confidence in the justice of the nation's legal system, and perhaps some critical lessons about what things were truly important and what direction her life should take.

NOTES

1. "Address by a Slave Mother," New York *Tribune*, September 7, 1853, p. 5.

2. For the material on Isabella's struggle with Peter, see Olive Gilbert, *Narrative of Sojourner Truth, a Northern Slave* (Boston: J. B. Yerrington and Son, Printers, 1850), pp. 74–79.

3. Ibid., pp. 86–87.

4. Ibid., p. 91.

5. Ibid., pp. 93–94.

6. Ibid., p. 69.

Chapter 4

GO YE INTO ALL THE WORLD

Not being one to allow a setback to set her down, Isabella took on any and every odd job she could find. But try as she might, no amount of effort seemed sufficient to allow her to do more than make ends meet. Far from being a path to financial security for the present and for her later years, New York had proven only to be a treadmill, on which her running feet took her nowhere—or worse. There she had nearly lost her son to the streets; there she had fallen into a religious scheme ending in ominous legal entanglements that threatened to blemish her good name; there she had become so focused on her own wants and needs that she had become insensitive to the needs of others in her same impoverished condition. Now disillusioned with the city and its feverish drive for money and material things, as well as with her sense that she had descended to its level, she appealed to her God for direction:

> I cried, "Lord, what wilt Thou have me to do?" And it came to me, "Go out of the city." And I said, "I will go just; just go." And that night—it was night—I said, "Lord, whither shall I go?" And the voice came to me just as plain as my own now. "Go east."[1]

So Isabella accepted the directive to leave. It was a bold decision in many ways. She would travel east, though she had never been east and knew no one there; she had no financial resources for such an venture, so would have to depend on what the generosity of others would open up to her; her mission would be to *lecture*, though she had always previously felt herself to be "ignorant" and inconsequential in the face of the white world of learning, power, and social status. Perhaps she had gotten the courage to step out before the world in this way as a result of two successful challenges in the public courts. By lecture she meant bearing witness to her faith in Jesus and urging others to leave their lives of sin to follow him. Perhaps she had developed that evangelistic message in her forays with Miss Gear to reclaim the lives of prostitutes and other social casualties. Nor was such a mission of wandering the highways and byways as a lone woman without its dangers, particularly for a black woman in an era and a place that still was rife with anti-black feelings. But Isabella had made up her mind that New York was in her history but not her future. And as to her security on the way, she firmly trusted that her God would protect and provide for her. Expecting that concerned family and friends would try to dissuade her, she kept her plans to herself until the time she had set to leave. When that time came, she informed the woman with whom she had been living, Mrs. Whiting, of her intended departure and that from then on she would have a new name, Sojourner. The woman's response was,

> "Where are you going." "Going east." Said she, "What does that mean?" The Lord has directed me to go east and leave this city at once." Said she, "Belle, you are crazy." "No, I ain't." And she said to her husband, "Why, Belles crazy." Said he, "I guess not." "But I tell you she is; she says she is going to have a new name, too. Don't that look crazy?" "Oh no," he said; and he urged me to have breakfast. But I would not stay.[2]

And so, on the morning of June 1, 1843, carrying but a change of clothing in a pillowcase, a little basket of food, and 25 cents in cash, given to her by a man in a prayer meeting, Sojourner reprised her daybreak walk from enslavement to freedom with a sunlit march from the snares of urban degradation to a liberty whose meanings she could not foresee but which she felt compelled to explore.

Setting out across Long Island, guided, as she believed, by the Spirit of God, Sojourner lodged at whatever place would receive her, free or at a cost. When her material resources ran low, she would accept offers of employment, but she refused payment of any more than was necessary to meet her minimal needs, regardless of how generous an employer sought to be in gratitude for her service. It seems she truly had written off the life of worldly things, in favor of a self-renouncing commitment to her religious mission.

By this point, it appears that a significant detail is added to the identity of the remarkable centerpiece of this story, though exactly how it came about is not clear. The transition from a woman establishing a stable, economically modest but secure life for self and family, grounded in a fervent religious faith, to a woman on a mission for God was marked by a change of personal name from Isabella to Sojourner. But history knows this woman as *Sojourner Truth*. What circumstance explains this dual new name? In the course of her subsequent life, she gave differing accounts, with explanations that seem to demonstrate how issues of memory can color reality. The first account was recorded by Harriet Beecher Stowe, the renowned 19th-century antislavery novelist, author of *Uncle Tom's Cabin*. In 1853, Truth told Stowe:

> When I left the house of bondage, I left everything behind. I wasn't going to keep nothin' of Egypt on me, and so I went to the Lord and asked Him to give me a new name. And the Lord gave me Sojourner, because I was to travel up and down the land, showin' the people their sins, and bein' a sign unto them. Afterward I told the Lord I wanted another name, 'cause everybody else had two names; and the Lord gave me Truth, because I was to declare the truth to the people.[3]

This explanation is believable enough and is consistent with what was happening in Truth's life. What is unclear, though, is what she meant by "When I left the house of bondage," and what was the content of the "Truth" that this name symbolized. She assumed the new name Sojourner when leaving New York, where she seems to have felt herself to have fallen into the bondage of the degraded urban life. But the quote associates "house of bondage" with Egypt, which more typically was used by the formerly enslaved as a metaphor for slavery.

And it was common for blacks, once free, to throw off the names they used in slavery; they understandably wanted "nothing of Egypt left on them." Yet, 1843, when the name was supposedly adopted, was 16 years after slavery ended for Truth, and it was several years before she took up abolition of slavery as a focus of her mission, which she saw initially as an evangelistic effort to bring people into faithful Christian living. Reminiscing on her name change in the latter years of her life, Truth added these details. Of the name Sojourner, she said, "It came to me like a telegraph dispatch to my brain, and God made my brain." Not being clear as to whether this occurred before or after departing New York, the name at least was reaffirmed to her after she left. She gave this account:

> I went down to the boat and over to Brooklyn, just a landing place then. I paid my fare out of the twenty-five cents and started on afoot with my pillow case. As I started, it came to me that my name was Sojourner. "There," said I to myself; the name has come, and I walked on about four miles, and I felt a little hungry, and a Quaker lady gave me a drink of water, asking me my name. . . . "What is thy name," said she. Said I, "Sojourner." "Where does thee get such a name as that." Said I, "The Lord has given it to me." "Thee gavest it to thyself, didn't thee?" said she, "and not the Lord; hast that been thy name long?" Said I, "No." "What was thy name?" "Belle." "Belle what?" "Whatever my master's name was." "Well, you say your name is Sojourner." "Yes, sir." "Sojourner what?" Well, I confessed I hadn't thought of that; and thereupon she picked that name to pieces and made it look so different that I said, "It don't seem to be such a name after all." But I said I must go, and replied pettishly that I couldn't tell where my friends were until I got there. And so I plodded on over the sandy road and was very hot and miserable. And in my wretchedness I said: "Oh God, give me a name with a handle to it; Oh that I had a name with a handle to it." And it came to me in that moment, dear chile, like a voice, just as true as God is true, "Sojourner *Truth*," and I LEAPED FOR JOY—SOJOURNER TRUTH!
>
> "Why," said I, "thank you God; that is a good name; Thou art my last master, and Thy name is Truth, and Truth shall be

my abiding name till I die. I had before had five other masters, and at the age of over forty, and the mother of five children. I was liberated."[4]

This rendering of the name's origin also has plausibility. It varies somewhat from the other cited account, though it does not necessarily contradict it. It adds detail and accurately indicates Truth's age at the time of the change. It may not be possible to sort out, conclusively, the complicated pieces of how this striking name, Sojourner Truth, came about. But for certain, it was an accurate characterization of the life that burst forth upon the national stage in the mid-19th century.

Truth's was a path-breaking mission. The social conventions of the day decreed that it was out of the natural order for women to engage in public speaking, and especially preaching, and more especially to audiences mixed with women and men. The podium and the pulpit were reserved for men only. A few black women had taken up traveling evangelism, with or without church approval. But it would be 10 years before the first woman would be ordained to preach, and more than a hundred years before U.S. denominations would begin officially authorizing women's ordination as a general practice. Truth, though, did not feel bound by social convention or the lack of church authorization. Nor was she dissuaded by what others, even significant others, might think of her actions. For instance, she rightly anticipated that her children would be concerned and would not approve. When they learned of her activities, they concluded that she must have lost her mind, that she had become, in her biographer's words, a "wandering maniac."[5] She claimed divine authorization and trusted divine support for the work to which she felt irresistibly drawn And so, as she went forward and encountered religious meetings along the way, she would give her "lecture," as allowed. Later, she began advertising to hold her own meetings, which drew increasingly large crowds.

By August, Truth had left New York State and traveled, by boat, to Connecticut. Continuing her trek, lecturing and working to earn her keep, she settled in for a stay at the city of New Haven. There she continued her practice of lecturing at meetings she called for herself, as well as those sponsored by others. The special appeal that Truth brought to her lecturing was the uniqueness of her developing religious ideas. The concepts she had received from Mau-mau Bett, from teachings in the white and black Methodist churches, and from her dialogues with other believers were filtered through her own thought patterns and religious intuitions. What was emerging was an array of beliefs that affirmed a Christianity based in a relationship with its central figure, Jesus, but that brought thoughtful, critical new perspectives on many of the traditional biblical interpretations and doctrines of that faith. As a result, audiences were intrigued by her lectures and became her promoters. For instance, one woman who heard her speak in New Haven invited her to Bristol so that friends there could hear her ideas. And from Bristol she was invited to Hartford by a man who wanted his friends there to hear her "new views and original opinions."[6] Truth was all too happy to accept these opportunities to carry out her mission.

The letter of introduction given to her to carry to Hartford is revealing of the impact her religious ideas was making on her hearers, an impact that overcame any social objections based on her race or her gender or her social status that might otherwise have disqualified her from access to a public platform. One can see in the letter, also, though, the impact of Truth's own personal character and genuineness of spirit:

> Sister,—I send you this living messenger, as I believe her to be one that God loves. Ethiopia is stretching forth her hands unto God. You can see by this sister, that God does by his Spirit alone teach his own children things to come. Please receive her, and she will tell you some new things. Let her tell her story without interrupting her, and give close attention, and you will see she has got the lever of truth, that God helps her to pry where but few can. She cannot read or write, but the law is in her heart.
>
> Send her to brother—, brother—, and where she can do the most good.
>
> From your brother, H.L.B.[7]

Truth truly trusted her own insights. Because she could not read, she was dependent upon others to read for her the primary Christian text, the Bible. But when they read, she wanted no commentary on the verses from the readers, no explanation of what the text supposedly meant. She only wanted to hear the words, themselves, from which she preferred to draw her own conclusions about their meanings. That's why she finally resorted to asking only children to read the Bible to her, since adults invariably took the occasion to add their own interpretations when asked to reread a passage, whereas children would do simply as they were asked, that is, to repeat verbatim the words on the page. Truth even asserted the belief that while the Bible did contain the word of God, the authors in that book had couched God's word in their own interpretations. So her approach was to *listen for the word of God* within the scriptures when they were read, rather than assuming the words printed and read *were* the actual word of God.

In Hartford, Truth introduced into her lecture profile an element that later would prove to be pivotal to her success. Persons who gathered to hear her speak also got to hear her sing. Hers was a strong, commanding voice—unpolished, unrefined, but compelling in its rich, deep tones that were rendered with the passion and gusto that she brought to all that she did. It became a key feature attracting people to meetings where she was announced as a speaker.

It was also at Hartford that Truth encountered a test of her ability to stand her ground in theological debate with learned clergy and laypersons. At this time in the United States, several religious groups had formed around the belief in an approaching "Second Advent," that Jesus would soon return to earth to bring destruction to the wicked and deliverance to the righteous. One such group, the Millerites, predicted 1843, that very year, as the beginning of the time in which this event would take place. Truth came in contact with persons holding such beliefs and attended two of their camp meetings, outdoor religious services of people from all around the region. At the second, she found that many among the worshippers were distressed over what their fate would be when Jesus came back. After listening intently to get the full flavor of their ideas, Truth stood upon a tree stump and began to speak to several who had gathered in one part of the campground. She urged them to calm themselves, lower their anxiety, and go to their tents and follow the biblical advice to "watch and pray." They accepted her direction. Then she went to where the preachers were expounding on the Second Advent doctrines. Having heard all she needed or wanted to hear, she then challenged the preachers, saying that their idea of Jesus's mass destruction of supposedly wicked humans did not seem like a sight that anyone should look forward to seeing. Furthermore, she said, if Jesus was going to burn the wicked to ashes, why should they allow their people to worry about that.

> If the Lord comes and burns—as you say he will—I am not going away; I am going to stay here and *stand the fire*, like Shadrach, Meshach, and Abednego! And Jesus will walk with me through the fire, and keep me from harm. . . . Do you tell me God's children *can't stand fire*.[8]

Caught off guard and without a ready defense against this challenge to their teachings, the clergy responded with questions of their own to Truth and with scripture verses chosen as supports to their positions. But after further conversation with her, they concluded that though she did not have adequate knowledge specifically about Second Adventism, she nonetheless possessed knowledge and insights at an unusual level that they could not dismiss.

Truth's performance at this Hartford camp meeting led to invitations to visit other towns. Accepting one to the manufacturing town of Cabotville, in Massachusetts, she spent a week or so there and then set out walking to Springfield, Massachusetts, where she thought her next lodging place might be. Perhaps she could settle there for a while, she thought, given that she had done much traveling since leaving New York, most of it walking. Stopping at a house along the way to ask for some bread to eat, the householders granted her request, but they recognized her from the camp meeting and asked if she would lead a meeting that night. She agreed. Several friends and neighbors were invited and Truth satisfied their expectations to hear one of her unique lectures. An added benefit for her was that some of the persons at the meeting were from Springfield, and they invited her to come and spend time in their homes, which she did.

The stay at Springfield lasted several months, the time Truth had hoped for, to rest her body and get her thoughts together for the continuation of her mission. When her provisions ran low, she worked at odd jobs, accepting no money but payment only in the things she needed to live on. Otherwise, she spent her time discussing religious matters with her new Springfield acquaintances and speaking at their meetings, deeply impressing her audiences as, according to one of her hosts, "her commanding figure and dignified manner hushed every trifler into silence, and her singular and sometimes uncouth modes of expression never provoked a laugh, but often were the whole audience melted into tears by her touching stories."[9] And as she discovered at Hartford, her gift for singing made her a special attraction, supported by her ability to offer moving prayers and to express her unique religious ideas in ways that audiences found fresh and provocative. Then, one other recollection of a host captured what would come to be the thread running through all of Truth's subsequent efforts in the public arena. As they were walking one day, Truth shared with her friend her frequent thought that "what a beautiful world this would be, when we should see everything right side up. Now, we see everything topsy-turvy, and all is confusion."[10] It was in pursuit of this vision of a world turned right side up that Truth was increasingly, and then consistently, to exert the force of her multigifted being.

FINDING HOME

Well into the winter of 1844, Truth's Springfield hosts took her to visit the Northampton Association of Education and Industry. She had thought of exploring a residence in one of the Shaker villages or at the noted Fruitlands settlement, but her Springfield friends may have thought the inclusive, antislavery orientation at Northampton would be more to her liking. There were even stations of the Underground Railroad in the area. Northampton was one among a number of utopian communities that were formed in the 19th century by persons seeking to live simple lives focused on the moral reform of society. This, of course, was well suited to Truth's vision, though initially she was turned off by the Spartan living conditions of Northampton and decided she was not going to stay there. But she discovered that many well-to-do, distinguished, broad-minded, socially progressive people had made their home in this racially integrated community, and that it genuinely functioned by values of equality and mutual respect for all, regardless of race or gender or class. So it seemed to her to be a place she could feel good to be part of, where she could set down roots and make for herself a home. While she had dedicated herself to living as

*Sojourner Truth's home on Park Street in Florence (Northampton), Massachusetts,
which she eventually shared with her daughters Diana, Elizabeth, and Sophia.
Courtesy American Antiquarian Society.*

God provided for her, through the charity of others, she also had come
to realize the importance of a dependable place to retreat to at the close
of the day, her own space, where she could rest and renew herself as she
saw fit. Northampton, then, would become her home.

And a fortunate decision this turned out to be. For at Northampton
Truth encountered some of the most prominent social activists in the
nation. George W. Benson, brother-in-law to noted abolitionist William Lloyd Garrison, lived at Northampton, as did black David Ruggles,
who operated a station of the Underground Railroad there. Garrison
himself lodged at Northampton for several weeks at a time. Here Truth
met Olive Gilbert, who would later publish *The Narrative of Sojourner
Truth*, one of the principle sources of information about her life. Another acquaintance made was Giles Stebbens, who many years later at
her funeral would offer tributes to Truth. It was also here at Northampton that Truth met the soon-to-be-famous Frederick Douglass, during
his visits to his friend David Ruggles, who had assisted Douglass in his
escape from slavery.

This community, as others like it, wanted to set a model for how
persons could live in democratic society without the ills of commer-
cial competition and the negative social practices based on class, race,

and other identity markers. Meals were taken together in a common dining room. Northampton established a high-quality school, open to persons both within and outside the community. It operated a silk mill to support itself, silk being chosen because it did not require slave labor. All persons were paid on an equal pay scale for their particular role in sustaining the community. For instance, Truth ran the communal laundry.

Northampton proved to be the scene for another significant test of Truth's religious mettle. After being there only a few months, she attended a camp meeting that was invaded by some young rowdies out to have fun through catcalling, hooting, and otherwise disrupting the services. The leaders of the meeting, being unable to persuade them to stop or to go away, threatened to call the police. But this made the young men more defiant. They went and gathered as many as 100 cohorts, continued creating noise and havoc, and even said they would set the meeting tent afire. The fear that gripped the crowd did not pass Truth over. She ran and hid behind a trunk in a corner of the tent, afraid not only that the young men would act on their threats to do the crowd harm but would start with her, she being the only black person there.

But suddenly, her convictions began to overrule her fear, as she asked herself, "Shall I run away and hide from the Devil? Me, a servant of the living God? Have I not faith enough to go out and quell this mob, when I know it is written, 'One shall chase a thousand, and two put ten thousand to flight?'" So she arose and beckoned other nearby leaders to go with her. They thought she was crazy to step out and were in no mood to join her. Going alone, then, she went from the tent to an elevated piece of ground and began to sing, with all her strength, a song of Christ's resurrection. The young rowdies began to gather, brandishing the sticks and clubs they had brought to terrorize the worshipping crowd. But far from using them on Truth, they listened to her sing. And when she stopped, they demanded that she sing more, offer prayer, and give religious testimony, promising not to harm her and, in fact, to do harm to anyone who raised a hand against her. She complied with their request. But she also sensed that beneath the raucous, antisocial façade these young men were asserting, there were lives of positive potential that could be reached with the right approach of one who cared. So she opened up to them in serious conversation, and candidly, freely answered their questions. In an amazing display of both courage and the ability to connect at a deep level across human boundaries, Truth had established a safe space for herself and a rapport with this formerly foreboding crowd, such that she could even say to them, "Well, there are two congregations on this ground. It is written that . . . the sheep shall be separated from the goats. The other preachers have the sheep, I have the goats. And I have a few sheep among my goats, but they are *very* ragged." There was much laughter. Then after agreeing to more requests for her singing, and now growing weary, she made the crowd a bargain: She would sing one more song, and they would leave the campgrounds. The bargain made and kept by both parties.[11]

Unfortunately, the Northampton effort at intentional, social-reform-based communitarian living suffered a short life-span, as did other, similar high-minded efforts that, like Northampton, ran into financial difficulties. In 1846, it ceased operations and dispersed its members. This was a great disappointment to Truth, since she had found a community she could believe in, where she was affirmed and respected. As she said, looking back on the experience in later years, "I was with them heart and soul for anything concerning human right, and my belief is in me yet and can't get out. George Benson, brother-in-law of William Lloyd Garrison, was one of them. What good times we had."[12] Truth went to live in the household of George Benson, who had been one of the Northampton founders, serving as his housekeeper. When, in April of 1850, some of the property of the Northampton community was put up for sale, many of it former residents purchased home sites. Samuel Hill, another Northampton founder, built a house for Truth in Northampton, near his own residence, and sold it to her for $300. Finally she had a home of her own, as she had longed for. She would pay for it by speaking fees and the sale of the book that Olive Gilbert, whom she had met at the Association, had composed from interviews with Truth, *The Narrative of Sojourner Truth, a Northern Slave*. William Lloyd Garrison wrote the preface for the book and arranged to have it printed. And though it is not clear how, and how often, she communicated with her children through the years, Truth did maintain contact with them, and, in fact, her three daughters, Diana, Elizabeth, and Sophia, the one she carried on her walk to freedom, came to live with her in her new Northampton home.

NOTES

1. "Sojourner Truth," Chicago *Daily Inter Ocean*, August 13, 1879, p. 3.

2. Ibid.

3. Carleton Mabee, *Sojourner Truth: Slave, Prophet, Legend* (New York: New York University Press, 1993), p. 45.

4. "Sojourner Truth."

5. Olive Gilbert, *Narrative of Sojourner Truth, a Northern Slave* (Boston: J. B. Yerrington and Son, Printers, 1850), p. 109.

6. Ibid., p. 106.

7. Ibid.

8. Ibid., p. 112.

9. Ibid., pp. 113–14.

10. Ibid.

11. Ibid., pp. 115–20.

12. "Sojourner Truth."

Chapter 5

BLOWING THE TRUMPET
IN ZION

When Sojourner left New York to inaugurate a lecture mission, her subject was faith in the biblical Jesus. She was intent upon drawing persons to a commitment to the faith in which she had been nurtured and then into which she had been dramatically converted. It was an evangelistic mission to "give account of the faith that was in her," following the appeal of the Christian scripture in I Peter 3:15. And up until her time at Northampton, that is basically the course she followed. Her speeches, her powerful musical testimony, her public conversations and debates were all focused on witnessing to her faith. Religious conviction is a powerful motivator, and spiritual conversion generates passion that mutes fear and confronts obstacles as things to be overcome, rather than insuperable barriers. And that was how Truth had proceeded.

Her experience at Northampton, however, seems to have introduced a new dimension to her mission. Northampton was not overtly a religious commune, but one that sought to apply what were the moral and ethical values of Judeo-Christian faith to the concrete issues, conflicts, and challenges of the world. As such, it did not call upon Truth to change her core, faith-based purposes but, rather, began to connect those purposes to the very real situations that constituted the narrative of her life, the story that drew crowds around her, even crowds of "young rowdies," to listen in rapt attention. Northampton's gathering of activists for equality and social justice lobbied through press and podium against chattel slavery, for women's rights, for temperance, for a vision of a society in which distinctions such as race, class, and gender were embraced and honored as contributions to the common good, rather than as points for social penalty and discrimination. They, and communities like theirs, rejected wealth accumulation for its own sake, conspicuous consumption of material possessions, and the economic exploitation so characteristic of the competitive capitalistic society they saw around them. Indeed, comments of some who observed the Northampton community included reactions to the seemingly contradictory sight of women and men from elite lifestyles of wealth and luxury having left that life behind for the extremely modest, even crude, circumstances of manual laborers building a community from the ground up with their own hands.

So Truth was stretched to expand the scope of her mission, and therefore of her lectures, by the modeling and influence of those she daily encountered. By 1849, whereas previously she might have been offering an exhortation to a camp meeting, she was now delivering a speech to the American Antislavery Society in New York City. One might wonder why or how it took over two decades beyond her emancipation from the deep abuses and cruelties of her own story of enslavement for the energies of her mission to be turned to this subject. The answer may lie in the complex ways that persons cope with deep trauma, such as slavery imposed on body and mind, ways that for some included an intentional leaving behind of that which was too painful to carry into the present. Truth had changed her name so that "nothin' from Egypt" would remain on her. For others, religious faith provided an alternative, positive sense of selfhood, affirmed by a source higher and greater than the world, as an antidote to the denigration and dehumanization of slavery. Those whose lives were thus "redeemed" might immerse themselves in this faith with a consuming drive to recruit others into its joys and benefits. One can see evidence of both these tendencies in Sojourner Truth's launch into a "lecturing" mission of evangelism.

Yet the relationship of the oppressed to their current and former oppressors cannot be so easily or simply characterized, just as the immense complexity of the human mind and spirit are not easily contained in simple terms. They defy attempts at logical categories and sensible descriptions. An example is Truth's journey in 1849 to visit the farm of none other than Mr. Dumont, who had exploited her labor and then betrayed his promise of her early emancipation. She went there to see her oldest daughter, Diana, who was still living on the property and bound to service to an aged Dumont, by the terms of the 1827 emancipation law. But far from the hostility and antipathy that one might anticipate, the encounter with Dumont seems to have been quite friendly. In fact, Dumont poured out to Truth a testimony of repentance for having engaged for so long in a practice that he now saw to be "the greatest curse the earth had ever felt." He said that in his day, slavery was hardly spoken against, so there was nothing in his world to show him its wrongs. Now the "sin of slavery" was voiced loud and clear from many quarters, so that no thinking, feeling person could miss it. Had it been so in his day, he said, he would have done very differently. Truth's response? "Oh, how sweet to my mind was this confession! . . . A slaveholding master turned to a brother! Poor old man, may the Lord bless him, and all slaveholders partake of his spirit."[1]

Perhaps as Truth gained more and more distance from the painful, firsthand experience of slavery she was able to get a perspective on it that made ever clearer how it stood in contradiction to the vision of life that her faith supported. For instance, when she discovered that in New York she had unknowingly been worshipping with a sister whom she had never known because of the family-splitting ways of slavery, her tearful response was, "Oh Lord, what is this slavery, that it can do such dreadful things? What evil can it not do?"[2] Thus, the overturning of slavery would surely be something that her mission must address. At the same time, while women might accommodate to their subordinate roles as the given order of things, in the 19th century they were increasingly pressing for wider recognition of their abilities and greater options to make contributions to the society. By 1848 the first women's rights convention was held in Seneca Falls, New York. Northampton modeled for Truth the principles the convention pursued for women, including them in the voting processes by which the association was governed. And of course, Truth's own brash, commonsense approach to social conventions could easily have led her to question the validity of prevailing gender restrictions. But however the shift in focus of Truth's lecturing came about, it was a shift that made of her a tour de force that would mark her as one of the most celebrated voices of her age for the causes of the abolition of slavery and the rights of women to full participation in U.S. society. These presented themselves to her mind as two faces of the same issue of justice and good moral sense. She would also add temperance to her list of objects for reform—the movement against what many said were the negative effects of the consumption of alcoholic beverages, another major reform concern in the 19th-century United States.

And so, in October of 1850, Sojourner Truth was on the speaker's platform of a women's rights convention in Worcester, Massachusetts, sharing the leadership with notable persons such as Lucretia Mott, one of the organizers of the Seneca Falls Convention. Frederick Douglass, himself a women's rights advocate, and William Lloyd Garrison, were also at this convention. Here, in her characteristically religion-based, cutting social challenge, Truth declared, "Woman set the world wrong by eating the forbidden fruit, and now she was going to set it right. . . . Goodness never had any beginning; it was from everlasting, and could never die. But Evil had a beginning, and must have an end."[3]

Left to right, abolitionists Wendell Phillips, William Lloyd Garrison, and George Thompson, all of whom encouraged Sojourner Truth's early lecture tours. Courtesy of the Trustees of the Boston Public Library.

The next month, Truth thrust forward the other prong of her assault on social injustice, speaking, along with Frederick Douglass and others, at the Fifteenth Annual Meeting of the Rhode Island Antislavery Society, held in Providence. At the center of concern of this meeting was the recently passed federal law mandating fugitive slaves found in the North to be returned to their southern owners. While other speakers may have voiced their dismay at this congressional support of the slavery system, Truth found in it an ironic cause for encouragement. By putting the unconscionable practices of slavery so clearly in view before the people, their moral senses would be awakened to action, leading them to join in active support of the abolitionist cause.

In these two back-to-back speaking engagements Sojourner Truth was immersing herself in some of the deepest social tensions of her day. It was considered an offense against social order, itself understood to be grounded in the divine natural order, for women to speak in public, especially to audiences where both women and men were present. Truth was advocating for women's right to participate in societal prerogatives that prevailing mores, backed by religious argument, reserved to men. She and the women's rights advocates were charged with campaigning for women, including, unthinkably, black women, to be able to "wear the breeches" with men and to "abolish the bible," the authoritative basis for the prevailing ender order in society.[4] And here one sees another tension point, the challenge to slavery and the subjugated position of persons of African descent. Alarmist whites saw in this an assault on the foundations of the nation and on biblical decrees concerning the proper relationships of racial groups, and as a ramp into social and biological "amalgamation," the one inevitably leading to the other. The editor of the New York Herald referred to the Worcester Conventioners as "That motley mingling of abolitionists, socialists, and infidels, of all races and colors" and as "fanatical mongrels . . . and fugitive lunatics."[5] Nor were these merely passive social tensions. Attendees at antislavery and women's rights meetings were often physically attacked and their offices and businesses ransacked. So to be a speaker at such events always had the potential of putting oneself in harm's way.

There were yet other tensions connected to these movements that Truth embraced. While the supporters of these causes typically saw them as complementary, as expressions of the same justice principles, they also faced the reality that members of the public might hold sympathy for one but not the other, and so by merging the two in one appeal, there was the risk of one cause being pulled down by the other. This led strategists on both sides to consider disconnecting the two into clearly separate movements.

In Truth's suggestion that the Fugitive Slave Law could prick the consciences of benevolent citizens and lead them to action, one sees a particular approach to social change, the approach of *moral suasion*. This approach was based on the conviction that effectively appealing to people's better selves, to their sense of right and wrong, to their religious convictions, to their sense of Constitutional justice, could result in their changing their problematic social behaviors, as well as changing the laws that undergirded social inequities. Others, though, despaired of such efforts, believing that discriminatory social practices and the values that underlay them were so deeply embedded and so resistant to change that moral suasion was futile, or, at best, required too long a time to achieve the desired result to be feasible. A more forceful approach was needed, from forms of coercive protest, such as boycotts, all the way up to armed conflict. Most persons, including most blacks, tended toward the former approach. Others, such as the white John Brown and the black Nat Turner, moved along the spectrum toward the latter. Actually, on into the 20th century and to the present, one can see expressions of these divergent approaches to social change. Frederick Douglass rose to fame as a moral suasionist, but the depth and recalcitrance of racial degradation and injustice gradually pulled him to explore force-based options. Sojourner Truth continued to believe that moral appeal, working on the conscience and through the legislative/judicial processes, would and empower the transformation. But she, too, came to appreciate the obdurate strength of oppressive forces and thus came finally to support the military action of the federal government in the Civil War.

Truth spoke at another antislavery meeting in December 1850, in Plymouth, Massachusetts, and then, the following February, traveled with British member of Parliament George Thompson on a two-month antislavery speaking tour of western New York. Thompson had gained high esteem among abolitionists for his efforts to end West Indian slavery. Originally, Garrison had planned the trip and planned to bear its expenses for himself and Thompson, inviting Truth to accompany them. Though illness prevented Garrison's travel, Thompson decided to continue the plan, still inviting Truth as companion, consenting to pay her expenses himself, and encouraging her that this would be an excellent opportunity to sell her books. And indeed it was so, as crowds gathered to hear her, Thompson, and the other travel partner, G. W. Putnam. Occasionally they were joined at meetings by Frederick Douglass. Truth was deeply impressed by the courtesies and acts of respect shown her by Thompson, as though he were oblivious to her status as a "poor black woman." Also she appreciated his generous, enthusiastic promotion of her book from the speaking platform. At the same time, Thompson and Putnam were deeply impressed with Truth as a public speaker, Putnam recalling after the journey that she "speaks with an ability that surprises the educated and the refined. She possesses a mind of rare power, and often, in the course of her short speeches, will throw out gems of thought."[6]

The speaking tour ended in Rochester, New York, where Frederick Douglass lived and from which he published his abolitionist paper the *North Star*. Here Truth struck an enduring friendship with Amy and Isaac Post, abolitionists, noted Underground Railroad conductors, women's rights activists, and leading participants in the new Spiritualist religious movement. The Posts provided lodging for Truth for the two and a half months of her stay in Rochester. Esther Lukens, an abolitionist from Ohio who was visiting in Rochester, had occasion there to experience Truth as speaker and advocate. In letters to the Ohio *Antislavery Bugle*, Lukens gave an assessment of Truth that, like the Putnam reflection, offers a window into the impactful presence of this self-effacing messenger of unanticipated truth, who spoke

> with an energy and overwhelming power that we might look for in vain among the most highly civilized and enlightened. Her heart is as soft and loving as a child's, her soul as strong and fixed as the everlasting rocks, and her moral sense has something like inspiration of divination.[7]

A LANDMARK MEETING

In spite of the joy Truth had taken in acquiring a home of her own in Northampton, it was not to that place that she returned when she left

Rochester. Instead, she traveled to Ohio, where she spoke at several antislavery meetings. Ohio, like many other northern states, presented a mixed picture when it came to the African American social condition. On the one hand, it was a free State, to which many an enslaved black had escaped. It was the location of Oberlin College, a pioneer in admitting blacks and women into enrollment. In Salem, Ohio, were the offices of the *Antislavery Bugle*, an active abolitionist journal. On the other hand, in the 1830s, Marius Robinson, who would later become editor of the *Antislavery Bugle,* had been attacked and injured in proslavery mob violence. In 1804 and 1807, Ohio had passed legislation discouraging black settlement in the state by requiring all blacks who wished to reside there to post a $500 bond guaranteeing good behavior. This sum of money was clearly beyond the means of all but a few blacks, and the decision to actively enforce the legislation in 1829 was cited by the National Negro Convention of 1831 as a reason for Ohio blacks seriously to consider relocating to Canada, where there were no such unfriendly requirements. So being a free state meant that for a number of possible political or economic reasons the official policy of the state prohibited the practice of slavery, but it did not necessarily mean that all, or most, citizens were opposed to slavery or that they thought positively about black people or welcomed their presence.

Ohio was also a leading-edge site of women's rights activities. One of the earliest women's rights conventions had been held in Salem, Ohio, in April of 1850. The association of these two movements for social justice was not coincidental. The women's rights movement was actually an outgrowth of women's activism for abolition. Beginning in the 1830s there was a flurry of antislavery organizing by women, including the circulation of petitions and abolitionist tracts. But their organization of antislavery conventions raised objections to women speaking before "mixed" audiences of women and men—a violation of traditional social mores. Women were confronted by an ironic contradiction: they could not speak out against slavery because *as women* they were not supposed to speak publicly. Their ability to address the social constriction of another group was blocked by their own social constriction. In the face of this realization and its potential to curtail a key component of the abolitionist strategy, a national women's antislavery convention in 1837 confronted the issue head-on. It resolved that "the time has come for women to move in that sphere which providence has assigned her, and no longer remain satisfied with the circumscribed limits which corrupt custom and a perverted application of Scripture have encircled her."[8] And so, meetings and conventions advocating the rights of women and an overturn of the traditional restrictions of their public functioning proliferated, emerging by midcentury in every northern state.

It was this arena of active but contested antislavery/women's rights ferment into which Sojourner Truth stepped in 1851 and made speeches that boosted her fame and became permanent attachments to her name. On May 28 and 29, the Unitarian Church in Akron hosted the Ohio Women's Rights Convention. Mrs. Frances D. Gage, president of the convention, opened the proceedings with a rhetorical flourish challenging male/female distinctions:

> Are not the natural wants and emotions of humanity common too, and shared equally by both sexes? Does man hunger and thirst, suffer cold and heat more than woman? Does he love and hate, hope and fear, joy and sorrow more than woman? Does his heart thrill with a deeper pleasure in doing good? Can his soul writhe in more bitter agony under the consciousness of evil or wrong? Is the sunshine more glorious, the air more quiet, the sounds of harmony more soothing, the perfume of flowers more exquisite, or forms of beauty more soul-satisfying to his senses than to hers. To all these interrogatories every one will answer, No![9]

But the flourishes that were to survive in the memory of that day came not from Gage but from Sojourner Truth. As president, it was at Gage's discretion who would be allowed to address the gathering. Writing about the convention in later years, Gage recalled the plea by some that Truth not be given the platform: "Again and again timorous and trembling ones came to me and said with earnestness, 'Don't let her speak, Mrs. G. It will ruin us. Every newspaper in the land will have our cause mixed with abolition and niggers, and we shall be utterly denounced,'" to which she replied, "We shall see when the time comes."[10] When the time came, Gage's decision was "yes." Truth did not betray the confidence thus placed in her. Gage recalled on that day seeing "a tall, gaunt black woman in a gray dress and white turban, surmounted by an uncouth sun-bonnet, march deliberately into the church, walk with the air of a queen up the aisle, and take her seat upon the pulpit steps."[11]

Gage reported that, on the second day of the Convention, the following scene unfolded:

> Slowly from her seat in the corner rose Sojourner Truth, who, till now, had scarcely lifted her head. "'Don't let her speak' gasped half a dozen in my ear.'" She moved slowly and solemnly to the front, laid her old bonnet at her feet, and turned her great speaking [sic] eyes to me. There was a hissing sound of disapprobation above and below. I rose and announced, "Sojourner Truth," and begged the audience to keep silence for a few moments. The tumult subsided at once, and every eye was fixed on this almost Amazon form, which stood nearly six feet high, head erect, and eye piercing the upper air, like one in a dream. At her first word, there was a profound hush. She spoke in deep tones, which, though not loud, reached every ear in the house, and away through the throng at the doors and windows:
>
> "Well, Children, where dar is so much racket there must be something out o' kilter. I tink that twixt the Negroes of the South and the women at the North all a talking' 'bout rights, the white men will be in a fix pretty soon."

Another recorded version of the speech has Truth saying that white men, in this circumstance, were "surely between a hawk and a buzzard."[12] In these opening remarks, Truth forthrightly spoke a prophetic word to the power center of the times, white males, challenging them to face up to the reality before them and respond justly, if only for self-interest. But then, Truth launched into the signature passage in the speech, the oratorical emblem by which she has become emblazoned on history:

> But what's all this here talkin' 'bout? That man over dar say that women needs to be helped into carriages, and lifted ober ditches, and to have the best place every whar. Nobody ever helped me into carriages, or ober mud puddles, or gives me any best place [and raising herself to her full height and her voice to a pitch

like rolling thunder, she asked], and ar'n't I a woman? Look at me! Look at my arm! [And she bared her right arm to the shoulder, showing her tremendous muscular power.] I have plowed and planted, gathered into barns, and no man could head me—and ar'n't I a woman? I could work as much and eat as much as a man (when I could get it), and bear the lash as well—and ar'n't I woman? I have born thirteen children an seen them most all sold off into slavery, and when I cried out with a mother's grief, none but Jesus heard—and ar'n't I a woman?[13]

In the rhythmic cadences of these remarks, Truth spoke out of the experience of the enslaved but championed her gender identity. She upended the 19th-century "cult of true womanhood" that defined "real women" as fragile, delicate, sexually chaste, and removed from the rough-and-tumble, harsh occupations of men in which they supposedly were incapable of functioning. Unable to *do* what men did, women, by implication, did not warrant the *rights and prerogatives* that men enjoyed. But Truth counterpointed the core premises of this differentiation of rights, asserting her real womanhood *and* her ability to do all that men did, and more. By implication, other women could too, if not arbitrarily restricted by men. Thus, she made an evidence-based (her own life record) rebuttal of male logic, challenging the assumptions of male social privilege and female subordination supposedly based on the superior male ability.

Some recent authors have questioned whether Truth actually used the "ar'n't I a woman" refrain, given conflicting reports of the speech published at that time. What is clear from all accounts is that she did deliver the essence of these remarks. Further, it is plausible that she would have employed such a phrase, since the women's rights movement had adopted as its motto "Am I Not a Woman and a Sister," an adaptation of abolitionism's rhetorical motto symbolically attributed to the enslaved, "Am I Not a Man and a Brother." The speech was referred to numerous times in subsequent years by other speakers and writers, each attributing to her that piercing refrain, more typically rendered, "Ain't I a woman?"

Truth then went on in the speech to address other comments that had been heard from the audience. Ministers of several denominations had come to hear what the conventioners were proposing and to inject their responses. Truth's answer to a clergyman's claim that men possessed superior rights because they had superior intellects was, "As for intellect, all I can say is, if a woman have a pint, and a man a quart—why can't she have her little pint full? You need not be afraid to give us our rights for fear we will take too much,—for we can't take more than our pint'll hold." If this sounded like an admission that women's mental capacity was less than that of men, it should be viewed in the light of a statement she made to Harriet Beecher Stowe in a later conversation: "Suppose a man's mind holds a quart, and a woman's don't hold but a pint; if her pint is *full*, it's as good as his quart."[14] She responded to yet another clergyman's claim in this way:

> "Then that little man in black there, he say woman can't have as much right as man, 'cause Christ wasn't a woman. Where did your Christ come from? . . ." Raising her voice still louder, she repeated, "Where did your Christ come from? From God and a woman. Man had nothing to do with him."

Her reply to the clergyman who pinned women's subordinate position on the sin of Eve was that even though she, Truth, could not read, she could hear, and she had heard the reading of scripture that said Eve caused the fall of man. However, "If the first woman God ever made was strong enough to turn the world upside down all her one lone, all these [women] together ought to be able to turn it right side up again, and now [that] they is asking to, the men better let 'em." After extended cheering from the audience, Truth made a gracious return to her corner, saying, "Bleeged to ye for hearin' me, and now ole Sojourner ha'n't got nothin' more to say." According to Gage, her applause-enveloped departure from the speaker's stand left "more than one of us with streaming eyes and hearts beating with gratitude. . . . I have never in my life seen anything like the magical influence that subdued the mobbish spirit of the day and turned the jibes and sneers of an excited crowd into notes of respect and admiration."[15]

Other women at the convention made eloquent speeches, reticent as they were to violate the norm against women speaking in public. But in convention president Gage's assessment, it was Sojourner Truth that carried the day. She exploded the predetermined definitions of gender and the presumed corresponding rights. She claimed the integrity of her own body as a site of respect and honor. She demonstrated the fallacy of the social prohibition of women speaking before "mixed" audiences of men and women, particularly as this was founded on the incompetence of the supposedly intellectually weak female mind to engage face-to-face the rational capabilities of learned men. She modeled the courage to assert and pursue convictions of equity and justice. Thus, in Gage's view, "She had taken us up in her strong arms and carried us safely over the slough of difficulty, turning the whole tide in our favor."[16] How ironic, yet historically consistent, that a poor, black woman should, in this public space, be credited with salving the fears, managing the crises, and nurturing toward full social maturity this representative segment of her white sisterhood, or her "children," as she addressed them. Many attendees purchased copies of Sojourner's book, her biography, which she regularly sold at such meetings as her main source of livelihood. They also extended to her multiple speaking invitations, satisfying indications to her of her lectures finding fertile ground and, hopefully, bearing fruit.

Over the next two years, Truth and her justice cohorts traveled the state of Ohio seeking opportunities to press their case for abolition. While the others usually went as a team, Truth preferred to go alone, though occasionally joining them in their meetings. Friends in Ashtabula County gave her a banner bearing antislavery and women's rights slogans. When she would come upon a camp meeting, she would display the banner, attract a crowd by her singing, then, with them in attention, preach to them and deliver her antislavery message. One summer, an antislavery friend loaned her a horse and buggy to use for her travels. This actually provided a window into how her religious faith continued to be a sustaining undercurrent to her mission. For in her journey through the state, when she came to a crossroads, being unfamiliar with the geography, and with no other basis to choose a direction, she would let loose the reins and say, "God, you drive." She reported that God always drove her to a place where she was able to conduct a successful meeting.[17]

One measure of her success was her finesse in handling audience interaction, including her ability to dissect and diffuse the arguments of those with whom she stood in opposition. What astounded observers of these confrontations was the way she often could do this with the framing of a question. As the editor of the *Antislavery Bugle* once wrote, "Sojourner Truth would sometimes throw in the way of politicians a most ugly difficulty—a whole argument, with premise, conclusion and application, in a single question." Noted abolitionist Parker Pillsbury, writing for the *Liberator*, said this was a skill for which Truth "is so eminently distinguished."[18] It was just this skill that Truth employed in a classic encounter with her friend but philosophical opponent, the esteemed Frederick Douglass.

Douglass had shared with William Lloyd Garrison a commitment to moral suasion as the road to abolition and the end to racial discrimination. But these social maladies had proven to be more deeply ingrained and persistent than Douglass had imagined. Increasingly, he came to despair of the white systems of power ever conceding black rights or living up to Constitutional provisions for blacks' equitable participation in U.S. society. The only alternative remaining, as Douglass was coming to see it, was for the enslaved and their supporters to take up arms to overthrow the oppressive system. William Lloyd Garrison, on the other hand, retained his allegiance to moral suasion, with a twist. Unlike Douglass, Garrison had lost faith in the Constitution, for he saw in it a clear acceptance of slavery and its supportive systems. Nonviolent moral suasion was the strategy to persuade the electorate to seek a rewrite of the Constitution as a document advancing universal freedom. In the meantime, Garrison, and those of like mind, argued against holding political office, since this was to participate in an illegitimate constitutional system. In fact, they advocated for dissolution of the federal union until it could be reunited under a valid Constitution. Sojourner Truth had come under the mentorship of Garrison, since the time of their meeting at Northampton. She shared his nonviolent, moral suasionist perspective on social change. And a classic passage from her account of one of her religious vision experiences demonstrates her critical view of the Constitution:

Children, I talks to God and God talks to me. I go out and talk to God in the fields and the woods. This morning I was walking out, and I got over the fence. I saw the wheat holding up its head, looking very big. I go up and take hold of it. You believe it, there was *no* wheat there? I say, "God, what is the matter with this wheat?" And He says to me, "Sojourner, there is a little weevil in it." Now I hear talking about the Constitution and the rights of man. I come up and I take hold of this Constitution. It looks *mighty big*, and I feel for my rights, but there ain't any there. Then I say, God, what ails this Constitution?" He says to me, "Sojourner, there is a little weevil in it."[19]

Truth did not side with Garrison to the extent of rejecting the Constitution as an unredeemable slaveholding document, or discounting the legitimacy of the Union. But she stood with him in the belief that appeals to the heart and conscience—moral suasion—was the stance that she would hold, as a critical thinker and as a believer in the power of the divine to change human direction. This would bring about the extraction of the "weevil" from the Constitution, leaving it fit as the national standard.

In August of 1852, Douglass was a featured speaker at the anniversary meeting of the Western Antislavery Society, in Salem, Ohio. In the course of his remarks, he argued his position that armed conflict was the only viable course of action for ending slavery's tyranny. As usual, Douglass's gift for stirring oratory lifted the crowd to fever pitch, at which point he posed the rhetorical question, which was actually a statement to seal his point: "What is the use of moral suasion to a people thus trampled in the dust?" But from the front row came the voice of Sojourner Truth, in startling reply: "Frederick, is God Dead?" The crowd was hushed; Douglass himself was stunned and speechless. One reporter who was present at the occasion wrote that "No bullet ever went to its mark with greater accuracy than that with which this interrogatory pierced the very heart of the question, and Douglass stood demolished and silent."[20] A single question, simple on its surface, evoked a complex of profound strategic and philosophical issues, particularly for a professed believing community. Is social transformation the result of human effort, divine intervention, some combination? What are the acceptable ways of dealing with each other in democratic community and of handling conflict resolution? Does the believer have the option of bloodshed while God lives? Will not God's justice ultimately triumph?

Daguerreotype of Frederick Douglass taken by Samuel Miller between 1847 and 1852. AP Photo/ Art Institute of Chicago, HO.

In later years, and facing different circumstances in society, both Truth and Douglass would moderate their positions on these questions. It was not the first encounter of alternative social visions between these two. Nor was it a clash of personalities or egos. These two larger-than-life figures on the national stage continued to hold each other in mutual respect and to honor each other's contributions to their common ultimate aims, while conceding that they must travel by different pathways.

WHAT TIME OF NIGHT IT IS

In both South and North, the quest for freedom and citizen's rights for the enslaved touched deeper and deeper nerves of animosity. So also did the push for extending full rights to women. Nowhere was this more evident than at the Women's Rights Convention in New York,

September 6–7, 1853. It was, in fact, the occasion of the first public demonstration of overt hostility to women presuming to transgress the boundaries of their assigned "sphere," the domestic arena, to claim the right to participation in public roles of leadership. Held at the city's Broadway Tabernacle, it drew 3,000 paid attendees, including some 1,000 men. The bulk of the men, egged on by negative press coverage of the convention, came to disrupt the proceedings. Their hissing, stomping, and abusive cat-calling were so riotous that the meeting became known as the "Mob Convention."

Sojourner Truth was present as a speaker for this meeting. True to her form, she stepped forth boldly to offer her remarks, conscious that in her person she represented the double essence of what the men so reviled: she was black and a woman pressing for women's rights. Ever perceptive of human nature, and impervious to the darts of irrational hatefulness that crowds might hurl at her, she launched right in to her scolding, extemporaneous speech.

First she acknowledged that her double identity was a lightening rod for their intense feelings, but that was good, she said, since it put the issues clearly on the table. She told them, however, that their unbecoming behaviors revealed problematic things about themselves that needed to be addressed: their hissing showed that "some of you have got the spirit of a goose, and some have got the spirit of a snake," two animals also given to hissing. In these remarks she was, perhaps, conveying that neither was she intimidated by them nor did their hostile masks conceal their true natures. Further, she claimed a legitimate right to speak to them because she was not an outside agitator but, rather, like them, "a good citizen of this State," born and reared there and feeling very much at home.

Then she went to the heart of the matter, drawing a comparison between the present and an "old times" situation described in the Bible. Queen Esther, in full knowledge that to come uninvited to address the king meant a death sentence, came forth, nonetheless, to press a case concerning wrongs being perpetrated against her group, the Jews. The king consented to hear her appeal. Not only did he hear her, but he granted her more than she asked, both saving her people from harm and also giving her "up to half of his kingdom." Women, the symbolic Esthers of today, have come forth amidst threats to their well-being to press their case against wrongs to their group. Surely today's king—the federal government—would not be "more crueler, or more harder," or less liberal, than the Babylonian king of old. And while that king ordered the execution of the perpetrator, Haman, and awarded Esther a material gift ("up to half of his kingdom"), women today don't desire any harm to men, nor any greater award than their basic rights as citizens.

Sojourner then confronted the audience with an element of shame implicit in their behavior. In obstinately opposing the request of women to have their personhood valued and their gifts included in the public workings of the society, men were rejecting and dismissing their own mothers, that class of persons whom they claimed to hold in highest esteem, and not just casually rejecting them, but doing so crudely and rudely with hissing and abusive language. What kind of home training did this exhibit, Truth asked, hissing and profaning their collective, symbolic mothers there on stage? "Sons and daughters ought to behave themselves before their mothers." So be it, though, Truth concluded. The resistance is deep and vocal.

> But we'll have our rights; see if we don't; and you can't stop us from them; see if you can. You may hiss as much as you like, but it is comin'. . . . Jesus says: "What I say to one, I say to all—watch!" I'm a-watchin'. . . . I'm 'round watchin' these things, and I wanted to come up and say these few things to you, and I'm glad of the hearin' you give me. I wanted to tell you a mite about Woman's Rights, and so I came out and said so. I am sittin' among you to watch; and every once and awhile I will come out and tell you what time of night it is.[21]

THE LIBYAN SYBIL

Following her convention appearance, Truth took the occasion to visit Harriet Beecher Stowe at her home in Andover, Massachusetts. The previous year, Stowe had published her famous antislavery novel *Uncle Tom's Cabin*, which had taken the nation by storm and would go on to be a major catalyst in the national debate that led to the Civil War.

Truth had observed the impact the novel was having and wanted to meet the person responsible for it, since its subject was the cause that was central to her own life's work. So she showed up, unannounced, at Stowe's home. Some 10 years later, Stowe published in the *Atlantic Monthly* an article containing her memory of that visit. As Stowe recalled,

> She was dressed in some stout, grayish stuff, neat and clean, though dusty from travel. On her head she wore a bright Madras handkerchief, arranged as a turban, after the manner of her race. She seemed perfectly self-possessed and at her ease,—in fact, there was almost an unconscious superiority, not unmixed with a solemn twinkle of humor, in the odd, composed manner in which she looked down on me.

The meeting began with a sort of appreciative mutual recognition.

> "So, this is *you*," [Sojourner] said.
> "Yes," I answered.
> "Well, honey, de Lord bless ye! I jes' thought I'd like to come an' have a look at ye. You's heerd o' me, I reckon?" she asked.
> "Yes, I think I have. You go about lecturing, do you not?"
> "Yes, honey, that's what I do. The Lord has made me a sign unto this nation, an' I go round-a-testifyin', an showin' on 'em their sins agin my people."

While intending to grant only a brief interview, Stowe found herself so taken with the unique and commanding personal presence of her visitor that she decided to call into the room the distinguished persons who were there visiting her, to extend to Sojourner an audience.

> "Sojourner, this is Dr. Beecher. He is a very celebrated preacher."
> "*Is* he" she said, offering her hand in a condescending manner, and looking down on his white head. "Ye dear lamb, I'm glad to see ye! De Lord bless ye! I love preachers. I'm a kind o' preacher myself."
> "You are?" said Dr. Beecher. "Do you preach from the Bible?"

"No, honey, can't preach from the Bible,—can't read a letter."

"Why, Sojourner, what do you preach from, then?"

Her answer was given with a solemn power of voice, peculiar to herself, that hushed every one in the room.

"When I preaches, I has jest one text to preach from, an' I always preaches from this one. My text is, 'WHEN I FOUND JESUS.'"

"Well, you couldn't have a better one," said one of the ministers.

Sojourner then went on to give a narrative of her life, intersected with the singing of the complete verses of a hymn about the glorious time that awaits the faithful in heaven.

The informal audience was impressed by the moving sermonic character of Truth's story and expressed the hope that they might hear her again. This apparently was Stowe's response, also, for she invited Truth to remain there for awhile as a guest of her family. The invitation accepted, the next several days were spent in mutually satisfying conversations on a number of subjects, from Truth's views on women's rights to the contents of her religious faith. Says Stowe,

> She would come up into the parlor, and sit among pictures and ornaments, in her simple stuff gown, with her heavy traveling-shoes, the central object of attention both to parents and children, always ready to talk or to sing, and putting into the common flow of conversation the keen edge of some shrewd remark.

A final sketch that Stowe provided in her article offers still another vista into Sojourner Truth's complex, multifaceted persona.

> There was at the time an invalid in the house, and Sojourner, on learning it, felt a mission to go and comfort her. It was curious to see the tall, gaunt, dusky figure stalk up to the bed with such an air of conscious authority, and take on herself the office of consoler with such a mixture of authority and tenderness. She talked as from above,—and at the same time, if a pillow needed changing or any office to be rendered, she did it with a strength and handiness that inspired trust. One felt as if the dark, strange woman

were quite able to take up the invalid in her bosom, and bear her as a lamb, both physically and spiritually. There was both power and sweetness in that great warm soul and that vigorous frame.

Then, Stowe added, wistfully, "At length, Sojourner, true to her name, departed. She had her mission elsewhere. Where now she is I know not; but she left deep memories behind her."[22]

Truth had, indeed, left deep memories in Stowe. During a trip to Rome in the late 1850s, Stowe visited sculptor William Wetmore Story, son of a U.S. Supreme Court Justice, who had established an art studio there. Story was working on a sculpture of the African queen Cleopatra. He became so intrigued by Stowe's description of Sojourner Truth and the narrative of her life that he decided his next project

William Wetmore Story's The Libyan Sibyl, *1860. The sculpture is said to have been inspired by Harriet Beecher Stowe's account of Sojourner Truth's life. The Metropolitan Museum of Art / Art Resource, NY.*

would be a sculpture that captured the essence of the fabled personage she described. He named the resulting work the Libyan Sybil, combining a reference to Truth's African heritage with the prophetess figure in Greek mythology that possessed the power to see into the future. The figure was exhibited at the 1852 London World's Fair, where it was widely acclaimed and greatly advanced Storey's reputation as a sculptor. At the same time, the association of this work with Sojourner Truth's name also enhanced her notability and public recognition. Between Stowe's 1863 article of the same name, and Story's sculpture, many came to refer to Truth as the Libyan Sybil. However, as one who knew Truth's bent of mind might have expected, she was not enamored with this literary recognition and grew impatient with reminders of it. As she once said to a friend, "I don't want to hear about that old symbol [Sybil?]; read me something that's going on *now*."[23]

NOTES

1. Olive Gilbert, *Narrative of Sojourner Truth, a Northern Slave* (Boston: J. B. Yerrington and Son, Printers, 1850), pp. 124–25.

2. Ibid., p. 81.

3. "Women's Rights Convention," New York *Tribune*, October 26, 1850, pp. 5–6.

4. "Woman's Rights Convention," New York *Herald*, October 25, 1850, p. 1.

5. "Woman's Rights Convention," New York *Herald*, October 25, 1850, p. 1, and October 28, 1850, p. 3.

6. Carleton Mabee, *Sojourner Truth: Slave, Prophet, Legend* (New York: New York University Press, 1993), p. 57, quoted from Boston *Liberator*, April 4, 1851.

7. "George Thompson in Rochester," Salem, Ohio, *Antislavery Bugle*, May 17, 1851, p. 3.

8. Digital History, September 30, 2010, http://www.digitalhistory. uh.edu/database/article_display.cfm?HHID=630.

9. The Library of Congress, Today in History, http://memory.loc. gov/ammem/today/may28.html.

10. Erlene Stetson and Linda David, *Glorying in Tribulation: The Life-work of Sojourner Truth* (East Lansing: Michigan State University Press, 1994), p. 111, quoted from *National Antislavery Standard*, May 2, 1863.

11. Ibid., p. 114, quoted from *National Antislavery Standard*, May 2, 1863.

12. Ibid., p. 118, quoted from *Antislavery Bugle*, May, 1851.

13. Frances Titus, *Narrative of Sojourner Truth; A Bondswoman of Olden Time, with a History of Her Labors and Correspondence Drawn from Her "Book of Life"* (Battle Creek, MI: Published by the author, 1878), pp. 133–34.

14. Sojourner Truth Institute, http://www.sojournertruth.org/Library/Archive/LibyanSibyl.htm.

15. Titus, *Narrative of Sojourner Truth*, p. 135.

16. Ibid.

17. Stetson and David, *Glorying in Tribulation*, p. 130.

18. Mabee, *Sojourner Truth*, p. 86.

19. Stetson and David, *Glorying in Tribulation*, p. 132, quoted from *National Antislavery Standard*, July 4, 1863.

20. Ibid., pp. 132–33.

21. "Document: Sojourner Truth: What Time of Night it Is (1853)," http://www.britannica.com/bps/additionalcontent/8/399825/Document-Sojourner-Truth-What-Time-of-Night-It-Is-1853#.

22. Sojourner Truth Institute, http://www.sojournertruth.org/Library/Archive/LibyanSibyl.htm.

23. Mabee, *Sojourner Truth*, p. 114, quoted from Detroit *Advertiser and Tribune*, January 11, 1869.

Chapter 6

A CHANGE OF LOCUS, BUT NOT FOCUS

Sojourner continued her lecturing throughout the northeastern states, diverting occasionally to attend to medical and other concerns in the lives of her three daughters, who had come to live in her home in Northampton. The Van Wagenens had purchased Sophia's freedom along with Sojourner's back in 1826. By 1850 Elizabeth and Diana, the oldest, had served out their obligated time of service to Dumont. When Sojourner purchased her Northampton home in 1850, she invited her daughters to join her. Book sales had gone sufficiently well that she was able to pay off the mortgage on the house in 1854.

In 1856, Quaker Henry Willis, whom Sojourner had met at an antislavery convention in Ohio, invited her to come to Battle Creek, Michigan, to address the Friends of Human Progress Annual Convention, meeting in October of that year. On this journey, she established several important contacts and friendships, including that of Frances Titus, who later would publish an expanded edition of Truth's biography.

The following year found Truth back speaking in the Battle Creek area. And in September 1857, she sold her Northampton property, at a considerable profit, and moved to Harmonia, Michigan, a community about six miles west of Battle Creek. Truth had set down roots in Northampton, so this was a major relocation. But several things may explain it. Harmonia was an intentional community, like both the Kingdom of Matthias and Northampton, which Truth had earlier found appealing. Harmonia was composed of Quakers and Quakers-becoming-Spiritualists. Quakers had helped Truth in her efforts to rescue her son, Peter, from his sale into southern enslavement. In Rochester, Truth had developed a deep friendship with Quakers Amy and Isaac Post, who introduced her to Spiritualism. Spiritualism taught that one could communicate with spirits of the dead for information about God and guidance in moral and ethical issues. It had emerged right in Rochester, scarcely three years before Truth's arrival there. Though it had several contributing influences, its origin is generally attributed to the Fox sisters, who were neighbors of the Posts and whom the Posts took into their home. Though Truth's deep religious bent and her practice of regular commu-

Sojourner Truth's eldest daughter, Diana Corbin. Sepia cabinet card. Courtesy of the Willard Library, Battle Creek, Michigan.

nication with God could have made her at least receptive to Spiritualist ideas, she might have welcomed association with Spiritualists as much or more because they, like Quakers, tended to be strong advocates for abolition and women's rights. Therefore, a Quaker/Spiritualist community like Harmonia (a term common in the Spiritualist world) would have been a comfortable and inviting environment for a person of Truth's beliefs and life commitments. Further, among the initial residents of the small Harmonia community were members of the Cornell family, Quakers with Spiritualist sympathies, whom Truth had known from her days of enslavement in Ulster County, New York, and who she said had invited her to come to Harmonia to live.

Truth was well-received in the Harmonia community. Her neighbors appreciated listening to stories of her life under slavery and enjoyed hearing her sing. The move seemed to have been a good decision. And just as in Northampton, Truth invited her family to join her in her new home. There is evidence that at least her grandson, the five-year-old Samuel Banks, did share this home.

ON THE ROAD AGAIN

In the early decades of the 19th century, particularly following the major slave rebellions from 1822 to 1831 and the heightened activities of the Underground Railroad, states in both the South and North began enacting laws, Black Codes, as they were called, severely restricting the civil privileges and the movements of blacks. The Black Codes of Ohio were referred to earlier; the 1853 Illinois Black Codes prohibited all black immigration into the state; the 1851 constitution of Indiana declared that "No Negro or Mulatto shall come into, or settle in, the State, after the adoption of this Constitution." Other provisions of the various states' Black Codes required existing black residents to register their presence with county officials and prohibited blacks from voting, enrolling in public schools, or testifying in courts against any white person, regardless of what valid evidence they may have to offer. It was against these kinds of social disabilities that Sojourner Truth was called upon to lend her voice in the fall of 1858, when Josephine Griffin of Indiana asked her to come and lecture on behalf of the 11,428 blacks living in that state.

At one of the antislavery meetings at which she was a speaker, at Silver Lake, attended by many proslavery Democrats, a rumor floated through the audience that Truth was actually a *man* in disguise. Dr. T. W. Strain, a physician, confronted Truth with this accusation and led the house to vote that she be required to submit herself to an examination by some female attendees to prove that she had breasts and was thus a women. This humiliating demand was but a stratagem to avoid facing the moral/ethical issues on which she was speaking, by diverting the discussion, avoiding the message by discrediting the messenger. The alleged fraudulent self-presentation of the speaker would excuse the audience from addressing the convicting substance of her speech. The deeper disingenuousness of the charge is revealed in the fact that "proving" to be a woman, her message would still be hastily dismissed because of the supposed offense of a woman addressing a mixed public audience of men and women. Perhaps lingering in the already dark shadows of this scenario was the specter of the white male's exploitative, sexual control of the black woman's body, so pervasive in the slavery regime and continuing well beyond. And perhaps this, aside from their own senses of modesty and gender propriety, also accounts for the resistance of the white women present to participation in this act, women who bore their own ironic experience of degradation as their white men elevated them onto a pedestal of "purity" while illicitly viewing and enjoying the bodies of black women.

William Hayward, who was present at the meeting, left this account of Truth's response:

> Sojourner told them that her breasts had suckled many a white babe, to the exclusion of her own offspring; that some of those white babies had grown to man's estate; that, although they had sucked her colored breasts, they were, in her estimation, far more manly than they (her persecutors) appeared to be; and she quietly asked them, as she disrobed her bosom, if they, too, wished to suck![1]

Far from this act of immodesty being to her shame, she said, it was to theirs for requiring it of her. Hayward recorded no expression of shame from those present.

A FINAL MOVE

By 1860, Sojourner Truth's daughter Elizabeth Banks and Elizabeth's husband had joined her in the house in Harmonia, along with their sons and grandsons, plus another of Truth's grandsons, James Caldwell. (James had accompanied Truth when she made her visit to Harriett Beecher Stowe some years before.) Eventually, though, Truth made another move, as, by 1867, the Harmonia community had broken up, its families scattering to other locales, and Truth, herself, purchased a home in Battle Creek.

Like Harmonia, Battle Creek offered an environment that Truth would have found appealing. For years, it had been a key station on the Underground Railroad, a transit point for the enslaved seeking to reach safe haven in Canada. The station was operated from the home of Quakers Erastus and Sarah Hussey, who over the years assisted more than 1,000 blacks in their escape to freedom. Erastus was at one time mayor of Battle Creek. This city was also the residence of many other Quakers and a growing center of Spiritualism. And though its population was not universally supportive of progressive social causes, it did have the reputation among some of being the most liberal city in the state.

Truth's Battle Creek place was a modest house. She had purchased a small barn on College Street from the Charles Merritt family and converted it to residential space. The Merritts were prominent Quakers whom Truth had befriended in her first days of speaking in the Battle Creek area. They had given her lodging when she was in town, and from time to time they employed her as a live-in nurse and domestic. The Merritts cultivated significant fruit and berry acreage and, according to one source, to earn additional income, Truth "would carry a tray, loaded with boxes of these berries, on her head to sell in town."[2] Before the decade was out, Truth's three daughters, their husbands, and children had moved into the new home. It was fairly cramped quarters for an extended family of this size. But it was what their resources would allow, under the continuing challenge of finding employment that would support a decent living. And it was to be the last home Truth would inhabit until her death.

NOTES

1. Frances Titus, *Narrative of Sojourner Truth; A Bondswoman of Olden Time, with a History of Her Labors and Correspondence Drawn from Her "Book of Life"* (Battle Creek, MI: Published by the author, 1878), p. 139.

2. Berenice Lowe, "Michigan Days of Sojourner Truth," http://www.sojournertruth.org/Library/Archive/MichiganDaysOfSojourner.htm.

Chapter 7

THOUGH A HOST ENCAMP AGAINST ME

In 1857, the U.S. Supreme Court, under Chief Justice Roger B. Taney, issued a landmark decision regarding the rights of persons of African descent to the protections of U.S. law. Dred Scott and his wife Harriet, held in slavery in the state of Missouri, had brought suit in 1846 against their owner seeking a declaration of their freedom. Their argument was that their former owner had taken them into the free state of Illinois and then into the free territory of Wisconsin, where the Missouri Compromise of 1820 had prohibited the practice of slavery. The Scotts claimed that by living in these free areas for almost nine years, they were thereby made free, and therefore, when their owner took them back to Missouri, he had acted illegally, having violated their free status. With the assistance of abolitionists and the financial backing of supportive friends, a case was entered in the U.S. District Court in St. Louis, which eventually ruled in Scott's favor. However, the decision was appealed by Scott's supposed owner and was tied up in the courts, continuing through an appeal, finally, to the U.S. Supreme Court in Washington.

By a seven-to-two vote, the Supreme Court justices ruled that the framers of the Constitution had clearly excluded all persons of African descent from the definition of "citizen" or "people of the United States." Thus, no such persons owned the rights of citizens to bring suit in any federal court because, in fact, the clear position of the Constitution's framers was that persons of African descent had "no rights which the white man was bound to respect." Furthermore, Congress did not have the authority to regulate the practice of slavery in the territories and, hence, the Missouri Compromise, on which the Scotts largely based their claim to freedom, was unconstitutional. The Scott's case, therefore, was denied.

Despite its obvious setback to black rights, Frederick Douglass saw in the Supreme Court's decision a positive aspect, in that it clearly exposed the depth and breadth of the black rights/black slavery issue for all to see. Most abolitionists, however, were outraged. So, also, were those northerners who were hoping to maintain the balance of political power between the free North and the slave South. The Dred Scott

Sojourner Truth in 1864. AP Photo/Library of Congress.

decision essentially opened the door for all present and subsequent territories to enter the Union as slave states. It so touched the increasingly raw social and political nerve endings of the nation that it became one of the chief precipitating forces of the Civil War, erupting scarcely three years later.

There is no record known of Sojourner Truth's specific response to the Dred Scott decision. She had offered her analogy that, like bug-infested wheat, the U.S. Constitution, with its exemplary principles of justice and freedom but with its explicit support of slavery, "had a little weevil in it." And on another occasion she offered her judgment that those who honored the Fugitive Slave Act of 1850 by seizing the enslaved who had escaped and returning them to slavery "don't know God." And so, one can project that she would have been deeply disturbed by this turn of events. But she had forged ahead with her mission of lecturing against society's denial of human rights and human freedom.

THE ONSET OF WAR

Even after the onset of the Civil War, in a very proslavery, hostile Indiana environment, Truth defiantly continued her lecturing. At one meeting in Angola, in 1862, proslavery Democrats threatened to burn down the building where she was scheduled to speak. Her response to this threat was, "Then I will speak upon the ashes." She went ahead with the meeting, as scheduled, escorted by troops of the Indiana Home Guard, who technically had "arrested" her so as to have her under their protection. Friends encouraged her to take along a sword or pistol, but she replied, "I carry no weapon; the Lord will reserve [preserve] me without weapons. I feel safe even in the midst of my enemies; for the truth is powerful and will prevail." In keeping with the Black Codes excluding blacks from the state, Truth, and others who hosted her for speaking events were arrested on different occasions and brought to trial. But each case ended in acquittal.[1]

Back in her Battle Creek home after the Indiana tour, Truth fell ill for several weeks in the winter and spring of 1863. The editor of the *Antislavery Standard* printed an appeal for donations to help with her medical and living expenses. It was a source of affirmation and delight that contributions came in from as far away as Ireland.

Her strength recovered, Truth collected supplies of food from friends
and merchants in the Battle Creek area and traveled to Detroit to provide a Thanksgiving dinner for the First Michigan Regiment of Colored Soldiers, stationed there at Camp Ward. Truth took great pride in
black soldiers, who were defying the prejudices of white northerners
who objected to fighting alongside them and who openly expressed
the belief that blacks could not be effective soldiers. Her own grandson, James Caldwell, had enlisted that year in the famed Massachusetts
54th Regiment (whose heroic battle at Fort Wagner in South Carolina
in that same year was heralded in the film *Glory*). The troops stood in
military formation to receive her, and she favored them with a patri-
otic speech. Returning a few days later, she sang a song for them of her
own composition. Set to the tune of "John Brown's Body" (used also
by the composer of the "Battle Hymn of the Republic") its lyrics boldly
asserted,

> We are valiant soldiers who've 'listed for the war;
> We are fighting for the Union, we are fighting for the law;
> We can shoot a rebel farther than a white man ever saw,
> As we go marching on.
>
> (Chorus)
> Glory, glory, hallelujah! Glory, glory, Hallelujah!
> Glory, glory, hallelujah, as we go marching on.
>
> Look there above the center, where the flag is waving bright;
> We are going out of slavery, we are bound for freedom's light;
> We mean to show Jeff Davis how the Africans can fight,
> As we go marching on. (Chorus)
>
> Father Abraham has spoken, and the message has been sent;
> The prison doors have opened, an out the prisoners went
> To join the sable army of African descent,
> As we go marching on. (Chorus)[2]

One can readily see in the words of this song Truth's proud confidence
in the courage and ability of black soldiers, as well as her assurance that
the war would ultimately result in full emancipation. The song became
popular among black troops during the war years.

Truth kept up with the progress of the war. Certainly she had a personal stake in how it unfolded, since her grandson had been captured by Confederate troops following the Fort Hood campaign and was being held prisoner. She had learned through him, among other sources, of the brutal treatment accorded black combatants by Confederate soldiers, whether taken captive or massacred in the aftermath of a battle. Perhaps an even broader stake, though, was her belief that this conflict would resolve what had been the germinal point of her own life story and a central focus of her mission, the harsh, chattel enslavement of a specific class of people, her own African-descended people.

NEW OCCASION TEACHES NEW DUTIES

As the Union troops advanced, blacks in their line of march would escape from their owners and flee to the Union camps, eventually ending up by the thousands as "contrabands of war" in makeshift encampments in the Washington, D.C., area. Such displaced persons, without material resources of their own, and being injected in such large numbers into the local economy, called for a significant humanitarian aid response. They likewise posed major financial and logistical challenges to the national administration. It is not surprising that Sojourner Truth, given her own background as once enslaved and now free and committed to the cause of black people, would want to go to Washington to see this scene for herself.

In June of 1864, Truth began a speaking tour that would take her, ultimately, to Washington. She was accompanied by her grandson Samuel Banks, the 14-year-old son of her daughter Elizabeth. Samuel provided travel assistance for Truth, would read for her, and handled her correspondence. After a stop in Detroit, she went on to Boston, where she met Harriet Tubman, famed Underground Railroad conductor. She and Tubman disagreed in their evaluation of President Lincoln. Tubman doubted that he was a friend to blacks, given his allowance of discrimination against them in recruitment into the Union army, then, once recruited, allowed their allotment of unequal pay, compared to whites. While conceding that these things were so, Truth focused on other aspects of Lincoln's leadership and on the great difficulty of managing all the complex dynamics of righting a misdirected nation. From Boston,

Truth fulfilled speaking engagements in New York City and New Jersey before finally arriving, by late September, in Washington. Along the way, she had lodged in the homes of abolition supporters, such as her New Jersey Quaker friend Rowland Johnson. In conjunction with her speaking, she had promoted the reelection of Abraham Lincoln, whose presidential leadership she highly regarded. She sold her biography and also *cartes de visite*—postcard photos of herself. As the caption on the cards said, "I sell the shadow to support the substance."

In Washington, Truth first stayed with Jane Swisshelm, who arranged for her to speak at benefits for the Colored Soldier's Aid Society. Truth also met Elizabeth Keckley, a gifted seamstress who had purchased her freedom from slavery and had become dressmaker and confidant to Mary Todd Lincoln, wife of the president. Keckley headed the Freedmen and Soldiers' Relief Association, an organization she had formed in 1862. Through this agency, Keckley and other black women extended aid to the thousands of contrabands in the camps, and they introduced Truth to the work. Characteristic of her, while she came to

FREE LECTURE!

SOJOURNER TRUTH,

Who has been a slave in the State of New York, and who has been a Lecturer for the last twenty-three years, whose characteristics have been so vividly portrayed by Mrs. Harriet Beecher Stowe, as the African Sybil, will deliver a lecture upon the present issues of the day,

At   On

And will give her experience as a Slave mother and religious woman. She comes highly recommended as a public speaker, having the approval of many thousands who have heard her earnest appeals, among whom are Wendell Phillips, Wm. Lloyd Garrison, and other distinguished men of the nation.

☞ At the close of her discourse she will offer for sale her photograph and a few of her choice songs.

Poster used to announce Sojourner Truth's speaking tour appearances. The location and date were added as needed. Courtesy of the State Archives of Michigan.

see, she soon found herself *doing* on behalf of those whose need claimed her response.

Keckley was also instrumental in another significant way. Truth held President Lincoln in high regard and wanted very much to meet him. She had seen other presidents passing in parade during her years in New York, but she coveted the chance to shake the hand of this one, whom she believed was God-sent. So she asked for help in arranging a White House visit from an acquaintance, Lucy Colman, a white abolitionist from Rochester, New York, who was in Washington teaching formerly enslaved blacks. Colman, in turn, sought the assistance of Elizabeth Keckley, who was able to make the appointment. On the morning of October 29, Truth and Colman arrived for their audience with the president.

Such a meeting was quite noteworthy, for although black slave labor had built the White House, it was far from common practice for blacks to enter its portals as invited guests. Truth told of the visit in two letters to friends, written during the three weeks after it took place. The November 3 letter was sent to her good friend Amy Post, in Rochester, New York. The letter reflects an interesting perspective. The description of the visit with the president is not prioritized; it seems almost as a "by the way." Coming first in the letter is Truth's account of the matter that brought her to Washington, her encounter with the freed blacks in the camps, and it offers some critical insights on how the camps were administered.

Mason's Island, Virginia, November 3, 1864

My Dear Daughter

And here I am in the midst of the freedmen, women, and children—and I am in a comfortable place here at the house of Ref. D. B. Nichols, Superintendent of Freedmen [at the government camp for freedmen here] and am treated very kindly indeed. I do not know but what I shall say here on Island all winter and go around among the freedmen's camps. They are all delighted to hear me talk. I think I am doing good. I am needed here. I see that the people here (white) [government employees] are only here for the loaves and fishes while the freedmen get the scales and crusts, and Mr. Nichols sees it too. . . . These office seekers tries to root

"I Sell the Shadow to Support the
Substance": One of Sojourner
Truth's well-known cartes de
visite, *which she sold, along with*
her biography, to raise funds.
Library of Congress Prints &
Photographs Division/LC-USZ62-
119343.

every one out that try to elevate these people and make them
know they are free. . . .[3]

Truth is pleased that she and Sammy have been comfortably housed
and well-received by the people of the camp. But she is deeply disturbed
by the callous treatment of the residents by the white government staff-
ers charged with looking after their welfare. Her initial desire to see the
situation of the camps undoubtedly had behind it the notion that she
could lend her assistance to them. Observing first-hand the pervasive
needs of the people did, in fact, open up to her ways that she was "doing
good" and was "needed" there. With no other obligations to prevent it,
she was now considering an extended stay in Washington to help out
the camps. Then, three-quarters of the way through the letter, Truth
mentions her visit to the president and gives a summary of what tran-
spired. Following this, though, she closes with a reference to her four
speaking engagements, two of which were benefits for the Freedmen's
Aid Society. Clearly, Truth is focused on the serious work at hand of

addressing the care for the destitute residents of the contraband camps, like herself formerly enslaved, poor, and needing advocates.

Truth's November 17 letter, to Rowland Johnson, deals more directly with her meeting with the president. Her words indicate that she was more than pleased with the way the visit unfolded.

Freedmen's Village, Va., Nov. 17, 1864

Dear Friend

. . . It was about 8 o'clock, a.m., when I called on the President. Upon entering his reception room we found about a dozen persons in waiting, among them two colored women. I had quite a pleasant time waiting until he was disengaged, and enjoyed his conversation with others he showed as much kindness and consideration to the colored persons as to the whites—if there was any difference, more. . . .

The President was seated at his desk. Mrs. C[olman] said to him, "This is Sojourner Truth, who has come all the way from Michigan to see you." He then arose, gave me his hand, made a bow, and said, "I am pleased to see you."

I said to him, Mr. President, when you first took your seat I feared you would be torn to pieces, for I likened you unto Daniel, who was thrown into the lion's den and if the lions did not tear you into pieces, I knew that it would be God that had saved you and I said if He spared me I would see you before the four years expired, and He has done so, and now I am here to see you for myself."

He then congratulated me on my having been spared. Then I said: "I appreciate you, for you are the best president that has ever taken the seat." He replied thus: "I expect you have reference to my having emancipated the slaves in my proclamation. But," said he, mentioning the names of several of his predecessors (and among them emphatically that of Washington), "they were all just as good, and would have done just as he had done if the time had come. If the people over the river (pointing across the Potomac) had behaved themselves, I could not have done what I have; but they did not, and I was compelled to these things."

I then said: "I thank God that you were the instrument selected by Him and the people to do it."

He then showed me the Bible presented to him by the colored people of Baltimore, of which you have no doubt seen a description. After I had looked it over, I said to him "This is beautiful indeed; the colored people have given this to the head of the government, and that government once sanctioned laws that would not permit its people to learn enough to enable them to read this Book. And for what? Let them answer who can."

I must say, and I am proud to say, that I never was treated by anyone with more kindness and cordiality than were shown to me by that great and good man, Abraham Lincoln, by the grace of God President of the United States for four years more. He took my little book, and with the same hand that signed the death-warrant of slavery, he wrote as follows:

"For Aunty Sojourner Truth,
Oct. 29, 1864 A. Lincoln."

As I was taking my leave, he arose and took my hand, and said he would be pleased to have me call again. I felt that I was in the presence of a friend, and I now thank God from the bottom of my heart that I always have advocated his cause, and have done it openly and boldly. I shall feel still more in duty bound to do so in time to come. May God assist me.

Now I must tell you something of this place. . . . I find many of the freedwomen very ignorant in relation to housekeeping, as most of them were instructed in field labor, but not in household duties. They all seem to think a great deal of me, and want to learn the way we live in the North. I am listened to with attention and respect, and from all things I judge it is the will of both God and the people that I should remain. . . .

Ask Mr. Oliver Johnson to please send me the *Standard* while I am here, as many of the colored people like to hear what is going on, and to know what is being done for them. Sammy, my grandson, reads for them. We are both well, and happy, and feel that we are in good employment. I find plenty of friends.

Your friend,
Sojourner Truth[4]

Truth appears not to have had a particular agenda for the meeting, neither lobbying for a cause nor making requests for presidential assistance. She was taken by the warmth and courtesy of the reception of her, a poor, black woman, by a person of Lincoln's stature—official public stature and stature in her esteem—"the best president who has ever taken the seat." Reflecting on the meeting some 15 years later, Truth said that in response to Lincoln's pointing to Washington and others as better presidents than himself, she told him that these others "never did anything for us; they may have been good to others, but they neglected to do anything for my race. Washington has a good name, but his name didn't reach to us. I knew well one of his slaves."[5] On another matter, she did not hold back her "signifying" commentary on blacks giving a book to the titular head of a government that had legislated against them learning to read the same. Nor did she hesitate to keep the president's perspective in balance by reminding him that in his bold emancipatory initiatives he was an "instrument selected by [God] and the people." But experiencing Lincoln in person and favored by his gracious reception, with an invitation to return, she was reconfirmed in her enthusiastic support of his national leadership.

It is a significant testimony to the genuineness of her commitments, though, that the "star power" of a president did not overshadow her concerns for the situation of the people on behalf of whom she had come to the Capitol. It is to them that her letter returns, in language that almost says, "Now, back to the real business at hand." And, as with the president, she locates her own anticipated work toward addressing their crucial, fundamental survival needs in "the will of both God and the people."

One indication that Truth's presence was proving useful to the situation of the camp dwellers was provided by the act of Capt. George B. Carse, the administrator of Freedmen's Village, a camp in Arlington, Virginia, in giving Truth and Sammy a rent-free cabin in the camp and a 200-seat adjacent building for use at her discretion. Capt. Carse described Truth's impact in this way:

She urged them to embrace for their children all opportunities of education and advancement. In fact she talked to them as a white person could not, for they would have been offended with such plain truths from any other source. I think she will do much good among them. She is one of them—she can call them her people—go into their houses and tell them much they should know. . . . She goes into their cabins with her knitting in her hand, and while she talks with them she knits. Few of them know how to knit, and but few how to make a loaf of bread, or anything of the kind. She wants to teach the old people how to knit, for they have no employment, and they will be much happier if usefully employed.[6]

Note the reference in Carse's comments to Truth knitting. One of her *cartes de visite* pictures her holding knitting yarn and needles. This skill can be traced back to her early years. In her days of slavery in New York, most women spun wool and knitted garments, and young Isabella would have done so for her various owners. She would also have done so as part of her domestic service in the Matthias and Northampton communes. For instance, the papers of the Northampton Association include a reference to Truth purchasing yarn. Knitting circles were common among the women in the abolitionist and women's suffrage groups in which Truth moved. So, in addressing the needs of the camp dwellers, Truth modeled for them this skill that was common in that day and sought to teach it as one means to be constructively occupied, and perhaps also to generate income.

If further proof were needed of the value of Truth's service to the camps, it came when, in December 1864, F. G. Shaw, president of the National Freedman's Relief Association, a private agency based in New York, appointed her as an official counselor to the residents of Freedman's Village. In this capacity, she continued the work she had already been doing, especially in teaching domestic skills and habits of cleanliness to the women. On Sundays, she provided religious leadership to large audiences through her preaching.

In her letter to Amy Post, Truth had spoken of the abuse and exploitation of camp dwellers by certain whites, some of them, for instance, selling to the residents clothing that had actually been donated to them. There were even more heinous abuses. At this time, Maryland was still a slave state. Slave dealers from there were in the practice of coming into the contraband camps and kidnapping children for sale into slavery. Unfortunately, this seems have had the collusion of the camp guards, because the kidnappers threatened the parents that if they put up resistance or raised an outcry, they would have them thrown into the guard house, and this actually happened in several cases. When Truth became aware of the practice, she impressed upon the parents that as free persons they had rights and could call in the law against the kidnappers. She urged them to stand up for their rights without fear of consequences. And she modeled her words for them. Whenever she saw a kidnapping in progress, she would scream at the perpetrators so fiercely as to frighten them away. When they threatened to have *her* thrown into the guard house, her answer was that if they attempted to do so, she would "make the United States rock like a cradle."[7]

Truth was just as fierce, though, in her efforts to usher the men and women in the camps into the full meaning of being free citizens. She criticized them harshly for their reliance on government handouts, which she thought encouraged laziness. She wanted them, instead, to learn to do for themselves and to adopt responsible, clean, disciplined behaviors. Knowing as she did the life from which they had come and the extreme limits on personal growth and skill development that slavery enforced, she realized that her goals for these newly free men and women would not easily be achieved. As she was quoted as saying, "Ah! Poor things; they have all to learn."[8] But she was willing to do what she could to make it so. The field of her opportunity was widened when, in September of 1865, the Bureau of Refugees, Freedmen, and Abandoned Lands, commonly known as the Freedmen's Bureau, appointed Truth to service in the Freedmen's Hospital to aid its administrator "in promoting order, cleanliness, industry, and virtue among the patients."[9]

"SOJOURNER PARKS"

In December 1955, Rosa Parks, a black seamstress living in Montgomery, Alabama, defied law and custom by refusing to give up her seat on a public bus to a white rider. She said of the incident that that day she was tired physically and tired internally of the demeaning segregative laws to which she had been bound to submit. Some 12 months later, following a protest boycott by the African American community, the Montgomery city buses were integrated, and the laws mandating segregation on Alabama buses were declared unconstitutional by the U.S. Supreme Court.

Ninety years earlier, as if déjà vu in reverse, there was a Sojourner Truth version of the Parks episode. The story unfolded in several segments. When Truth came to Washington, D.C., the city's streetcar system included a "Jim Crow" ("colored") car on each of its tracks. But if whites filled the seats first, as often happened, blacks could only ride standing up. After experiencing this problem, Truth complained to the president of the street railroad, which led to the removal of the Jim Crow cars. In so doing, the transportation company was complying with the bill introduced in early 1865 by Sen. Charles Sumner of Massachusetts, banning segregation on Washington's streetcars. President Lincoln had signed the bill into law on March 3, 1865.

Changes in laws, however, do not immediately change ingrained social behaviors, and blacks continued to experience discrimination and abuse when they attempted to ride the streetcars. On one occasion when Truth went to ride the streetcar, her attempts to hail a car were ignored by the conductor and the driver. Ignored, again, by the conductor of the next-coming car, she shouted so strongly for the car to halt to let her board ("I want to ride. I want to ride. I want to ride!").[10] that the car was blocked by people and vehicles that had stopped in response to the commotion. When she caught up with it and boarded, the conductor ordered her to "Go forward (outside) where the horses are, or I will throw you out." Truth dared the conductor to throw her out and added that she knew the law and was not intimidated by his threat. The conductor let her be. Sympathetic soldiers standing in earshot of the encounter were heard to tell other passengers, "You ought to have heard that old woman talk to the conductor." Seemingly pleased with the outcome of her challenge, she allowed herself a ride farther than her original destination, and when she finally got off, exulted to herself, "Bless God! I have had a ride."

On another day when her attempt to hail a streetcar was ignored, and when she ran and caught up with the car, boarded, and upbraided the conductor for shamefully treating an old lady thus, he threatened to eject her. Her answer was, "If you attempt that, it will cost you more than your car and horses are worth." This was apparently a reference to the consequences of violating the Sumner law. At that point, a military officer on board the car spoke up on her behalf, and she rode to her destination.

On still another occasion, Truth boarded a streetcar with a black nurse, on their way to Freedmen's Hospital, when two white passengers complained to the conductor about having to ride in the same car with these black women. They asked if "niggers" were allowed to ride in these cars. At the conductor's hesitant "yes," the women said, "'Tis a shame and a disgrace. They ought to have a nigger car on the track." But Truth answered them, saying, "Of course colored people ride in the cars. Street cars are designed for poor white and colored folks. Carriages are for ladies and gentlemen. There are carriages [pointing out the window] waiting to take you three or four miles for sixpence, and then you talk of a nigger car!" As the ladies got up to leave, presumably to take one of the carriages, Truth bid them a taunting "Good bye, ladies."

Traveling through the city one day with a white abolitionist friend, Josephine Griffing, Griffing hailed a streetcar, which stopped to let her board but then took off, intentionally leaving Truth behind. Catching hold of the car's iron rail, she was dragged for several yards before Griffing managed to get the conductor to stop the car. Reporting this incident to the rail company president, the conductor was fired. The president instructed her that she was to take the number of the car if such a thing should ever happen again and he would again fire the conductor or driver that mistreated her.

Finally, one day Truth and a white abolitionist from Michigan, Laura Haviland, who was working with Truth at the Freedmen's Hospital, had been going about the city to collect supplies for the patients. Deciding to take the street car for their return to the hospital, Haviland signaled for an oncoming car, but Truth pretended to keep walking, since whites traveling with blacks normally were not allowed to board. When the car stopped for Haviland, Truth jumped aboard ahead of her. Truth gives this account of what happened next.

The conductor pushed me back, saying, "Get out of the way and let this lady (Haviland) come in." "Whoop," said I, "I am a lady, too." We met with no further opposition till we were obliged to change cars. A man coming out as we were going into the next car asked the conductor if "niggers were allowed to ride." The conductor grabbed me by the shoulder and, jerking me around, ordered me to get out. I told him I would not. Mrs. Haviland took hold of my other arm and said, "Don't put her out." The conductor asked if I belonged to her. "No," replied Mrs. Haviland, "She belongs to humanity." "Then take her and go," said he, and giving me another push slammed me against the door. I told him I would let him know if he could shove me about like a dog, and said to Mrs. Haviland, "Take the number of this car."

The conductor withdrew and let them alone, perhaps realizing that he might be reported for his actions, the women having taken down his car number. When Truth and Haviland arrived to the hospital, they had Truth's arm examined by the doctors, who found that she had a dislocated bone. She filed a complaint with the railway president, who fired the conductor and advised her to seek his arrest for assault and battery. She did so and, provided a lawyer by the Freedmen's Bureau, the matter was taken to trial. The limited data available suggest that the verdict was rendered in her favor.

Truth was not alone in challenging segregation and abusive treatment of blacks in the public transportation systems of her day. David Ruggles, who had been a coresident with her in the Northampton community, had in 1841 been dragged from a train in New Bedford, Massachusetts, for refusing to move to the Jim Crow car. He unsuccessfully pursued the case in court. Another friend, Frederick Douglass, also had been forcibly ejected from Massachusetts trains for sitting in "whites only" cars. The black Rev. J.W.C. Pennington led New York City's blacks in a "ride in" campaign to desegregate that city's transportation system. There is no evidence that Truth intentionally acted in concert with these other efforts, nor that she, herself, intended her efforts as a "campaign" against segregation. But together, these separate initiatives brought to public attention the issue of black rights and public abusive mistreatment of blacks. They generated the pressure, perhaps including a measure of public shame, that resulted in the integration of public transportation in several major cities of that time.

Again, Truth's actions were not unique or isolated. Other black Washingtonians had challenged segregationist practices by entering whites-only cars or, after Jim Crow cars were banned, enduring white hostility, even physical assault, by taking seats in the legally integrated cars. But Truth modeled the courage to assert black rights. The black nurse with whom she rode the street car on that day had been cringing in self-conscious discomfort and fear as a black person in that "white" context. But Truth mentored her, by bold example, in claiming and expressing the legitimacy of black selfhood. Truth modeled the vulnerable exposure to the possibility of, indeed the actuality of, abuse and assault that have been shown to be the necessary condition for progress against endemic prejudice and social marginalization. Her actions stirred the waters and set the climate for the public to examine its actions toward transforming them. For instance, at least four of Washington's papers carried the story of the trial of the conductor that had injured her. She perhaps engendered the courage in others to do likewise and to step into the space of legal prerogatives that she had claimed for herself. As Truth gleefully reported, "Before the trial was ended, the inside of the cars looked like pepper and salt; and I felt, like Poll Parrot, 'Jack, I am riding.'" With even deeper satisfaction, she recounted that not long thereafter, "A lady saw some colored women looking wistfully toward a car, when the conductor, halting, said, 'Walk in, ladies.' Now they who had so lately cursed me for wanting to ride, could stop for black as well as white, and could even condescend to say, 'Walk in, ladies.'"

NOTES

1. Frances Titus, *Narrative of Sojourner Truth; A Bondswoman of Olden Time, with a History of Her Labors and Correspondence Drawn from Her "Book of Life"* (Battle Creek, MI: Published by the author, 1878), pp. 140–41.

2. Carleton Mabee, *Sojourner Truth: Slave, Prophet, Legend* (New York: New York University Press, 1993), pp. 117–18.

3. Ibid., p. 119.

4. Ibid., pp. 121–22.

5. "Sojourner Truth," Chicago *Daily Inter Ocean*, August 13, 1879, p. 3.

6. Mabee, *Sojourner Truth*, p. 120.

7. Titus, *Narrative of Sojourner Truth*, pp. 182–83.

8. Mabee, *Sojourner Truth*, p. 141.

9. Titus, *Narrative of Sojourner Truth*, p. 183.

10. Quoted material in this account of Truth's challenges to segregation in Washington's public transportation system is taken from Titus, *Narrative of Sojourner Truth*, pp. 184–87.

Chapter 8

SO THEY CAN BE A PEOPLE AMONG YOU

Following the close of the Civil War, the numbers in the contraband camps around Washington were swelled by returning black Union soldiers, as well as by new waves of freed persons. They were coming into the city from their former farm areas in hopes both of escaping the hostility of their former owners as well as finding better living situations. Instead, they wound up in cramped, squalid quarters, where families, often multigenerational families, shared space in tiny, makeshift cabins—"mere apologies for shanties, which are without light or ventilation," as one police official described them. "Here," he said, "crime, filth, and poverty seem to vie with each other in a career of degradation and death."[1] With limited skills, beyond those specific to their tasks under slavery, and with a local economy able to employ only a scant few of them, the destitution of the camp dwellers presented an enormous challenge.

The Bureau of Refugees, Freedmen, and Abandoned Lands, known as the Freedmen's Bureau, was an idea initiated by President Lincoln and authorized by Congress in 1865, largely through the advocacy of Sojourner Truth's friend Josephine Griffing. Under the direction of Gen. Otis Oliver Howard, after whom the historically black Howard

University was named, the Bureau was charged with aiding the formerly enslaved, as well as impoverished whites, through provision of clothing, food, health care, education, jobs, and assistance in reconnecting with family members. The Bureau was also given authority to administer the lands and property confiscated from the Confederacy. Many hoped that the lands would be redistributed among the freed persons as their fresh start to a viable existence. For instance, Union General William T. Sherman had issued an order that blacks freed by his troops be given "forty acres and a mule." (Though some received the grants, President Andrew Johnson later reversed the order; the lands reverted to their former white owners.) In spite of genuine efforts, but also in the face of intense opposition from former Confederates, the relief and support efforts of the Bureau were sorely inadequate, nor were the Confederate lands redistributed.

In Washington, the Freedmen's Bureau had established a hospital, distributed food and clothing to camp dwellers, and looked to provide employment opportunities, among other interventions. But the conditions in the camps continued to be a grave concern. Truth had been moved by those conditions to remain indefinitely in Washington to work with the public and private agencies, such as the Bureau, on behalf of the freed persons in the camps. But she viewed their interventions ambivalently. While appreciating the help provided, such as the food allotments that kept many from starvation, she also saw these provisions of charity as creating dependence and as stifling the initiative of these blacks to take responsibility for their own support and advancement. She was known to criticize them sharply for being content to receive handouts while exhibiting no aspiration to empower themselves. It was this uneasiness on Truth's part that led her to both a short- and a long-range strategy toward the goal of black self-sufficiency.

The immediate, short-term need of the people was to get out of the camps and into income-producing employment. That was one of the responsibilities of the Freedmen's Bureau, and Truth set herself to helping it to happen, working on her own and also in cooperation with Josephine Griffing. So, for instance, in July 1866, Truth wrote to her friend Amy Post in Rochester, New York:

I would like to know if you can find some good places [jobs and lodging] for women that have children. There has been a great many gone on to the west, but there are yet some good women here that want homes. These have all been slaves. There are some that have no children, also. I shall most likely leave here this month and take them along if you or some of the friends of the Cause would find homes for them.[2]

The letter reflects Truth's particular concern to preserve families intact. While many reform-minded persons were willing to provide employment for freedpersons, it was not unusual for them to request women to come without their children, or to request children only, or to specify single women. To satisfy such stipulations meant that families would be separated—a circumstance that Truth knew all too painfully from her own experience; or that young children would be deprived of adequate parental care; or that older persons in need of care and assistance would be abandoned in their need. The reference in the letter to taking the recruited women along reflects the provision that the Freedmen's Bureau made to pay the transportation costs of persons who were offered employment, and also the provision arranged by Griffing for the Bureau to pay Truth's expenses when she escorted persons to their placements. There is no clear evidence that this initial exploration of Rochester as a site for resettling contraband camp dwellers bore fruit.

Another site where Truth and Griffing sought to place camp dwellers for employment was Truth's own home city of Battle Creek. With the assistance of friends there, such as the Willis, Snodgrass, and Merritt families, she and Griffing transported 28 persons by train in 1866 to Battle Creek, as well as numbers of others to stops along the way. One of those on board, Payton Grayson, remembered that "Aunt Sojourner," as he referred to her, urged them to leave Washington because there was no future for them there. "[She] wanted to help us help ourselves. . . . That's the reason she had us to come to Battle Creek and small towns, instead of the big cities, so we could find work."[3] Grayson recalled that as the train moved through the Midwest, Truth would signal to the passengers the stop where persons were waiting to receive them into their new homes and employment. This was the first of many excursions either arranged by Truth or accompanied by her for bringing contraband camp dwellers from Washington to start new lives in Battle Creek and other midwestern cities.

Truth still entertained hopes, though, that Rochester, New York, would prove to be a good place to accomplish the same purposes. She was not alone, for already there were several resettlement agents of the Freedmen's Bureau working in Rochester and throughout the state of New York. When Truth visited her Rochester friends Isaac and Amy Post in March of 1867, they published an advertisement in local newspapers for employers for resettled workers:

> To the Public.—Sojourner Truth, the well known Mrs. Stowe's African Sybil, is now in Rochester, endeavoring to find employment for some of the Southern freed people, who are in Washington, several thousands of them supported by the government and philanthropists, in idleness. They are willing and able to work, but there is none for them there.
>
> It is therefore proposed to establish a depot for some of them in Rochester, where the farmers and citizens can supply their great need for help. They will be transported here without expense to the employer [the Bureau would pay for the transportation], but to pay expenses while in the city, fifty cents or a dollar would be required.
>
> We therefore solicit all who need help, and are willing to pay them such wages as they may earn, to immediately avail themselves of this opportunity, by writing to or informing Sojourner Truth, care of Isaac Post, Rochester; of what number and kind; whether men, women or families, they desire.
>
> On or before the arrival of these people, notice will be given in the city papers, that applicants may come and select for themselves.
>
> Sojourner Truth, who is the life and soul of this movement, intends holding meetings in adjoining towns, in aid of this effort.[4]

The advertisement brought a flood of responses from persons seeking both domestic and farm laborers, and in May, Truth escorted a group of persons to jobs there. Others were brought on subsequent trips. In August of 1867, Truth wrote to Post from Washington:

> How is Aunt Mary and the women I brought you getting along, and the rest of the women? I do want very much to know. And

how is the little baby of Mrs. Willis? It was so poorly when I came away. Did it live or die? I've bought me a lot with a barn on it and I'm going to fix the barn into a house and I think I shall be very comfortable & then I shall want you to come and see me.[5]

However, the number of willing employers far outstripped the number of workers the Bureau managed to send. Griffing wrote to Truth that several factors accounted for the shortfall, including the challenge to Bureau staff to handle the sheer volume of applications for workers and the administrative paperwork of the office; the negative image of the North conveyed to the contrabands by certain southern agents; and the hesitance of some persons to leave Washington, where they now enjoyed the right to vote, to go to states that still withheld that prerogative from blacks. Further, the Freedmen's Bureau, never liberally funded, was, by the summer of 1867, becoming increasingly strapped for the money to support its work, as southern Democrats pressured Congress to strip its already limited funding. As a result of the various factors, relatively few camp dwellers were actually dispatched to Rochester (or elsewhere). Many of those whom Truth escorted there she had recruited herself on trips to southern Virginia and perhaps as far south as North Carolina.

Sometime in 1868, Josephine Griffing's staff position at the Freedmen's Bureau was cut, and the life of the Bureau itself was on a steep decline. In 1870 when Truth visited Washington, the camps still teemed with freedpersons, destitute of means and idle of work. The goal of introducing the formerly enslaved to productive, self-supporting citizenship fell victim to a short-lived public sympathy for Reconstruction of the South and for the land reform that might have provided an economic basis for achievement of the goal.

Sojourner Truth had called upon the government to aid the freedpersons in part through education. And here the Freedmen's Bureau made its most lasting contribution. Some five million dollars were expended to set up schools for blacks, which enabled, by the end of 1865, more than 90,000 freedpersons to enroll as students in public schools, with attendance rates between 79 and 82 percent. From 1866 until it ceased operations in 1872, the Bureau, in cooperation with the American Missionary Association, established an estimated 25 colleges and normal schools for blacks, many of which remain in operation today, such as Howard University, St. Augustine's College, Fisk University, Johnson C. Smith University, Clark Atlanta University, Dillard University, Shaw University, Virginia Union University, and Tougaloo College, among others.

But as impressive as these accomplishments were on their own, they still left the great majority of newly freed African Americans with no avenues to a viable existence. And as to those in the camps around Washington, about whom Sojourner Truth had been so deeply concerned, they remained in what to Truth was a demeaning posture of dependence on government charity. She had devoted several years of her life and expended her personal resources to redeem them from that posture. She even used her own funds to pay transportation and lodging costs for those being resettled when Bureau disbursements were delayed, depending on the Bureau to reimburse her expenses, but she did not receive those reimbursements without significant interventions of others on her behalf. Thus, though she took some satisfaction in what little she personally accomplished, this short-range strategic plan for black self-sufficiency was not crowned with the success for which she had hoped. The relocation of freed blacks to the North did not prove to be the answer. So she shifted her focus to a longer-range strategy, in another compass direction.

LOOKING WEST

Sojourner Truth had long desired that African Americans achieve the independence and dignity and self-respect that would come from supporting themselves by their own industrious labor. This had been the path she had followed herself, from the earliest days of her self-emancipation from owner Dumont—rejecting charity and, instead, earning her support through conscientious hard work. Even when she had solicited and accepted donations to meet her expenses, this was always either in cases of her incapacity to work or as a means of freeing her up so that she could devote herself more fully to social causes she had adopted. Further, Truth perhaps saw farm labor, still the main source of livelihood of most citizens, as one way around the tenuous prospects of finding steady work in the cities. Thus we find her making this appeal in a speech to blacks facing employment issues in 1853 in New York City:

My colored brothers and sisters, there's a remedy for this; where I was lately lecturing out in Pennsylvania, the farmers wanted good men and women to work their farms on shares for them. Why can't you go out there?—and depend on it, in the course of time you will get to be independent.[6]

Even better than working someone else's land as the road to independence would be working one's own land toward that end. That was the hope held out for emancipated blacks by the *Anglo-African* editorial in November 1861, that called for lands confiscated from the Confederacy to be divided among the freedpersons, because,

> . . . [T]hey know best how to cultivate them, and will joyfully bring their brawny arms, their willing hearts, and their skilled hands to the glorious labor of cultivating as their OWN, the lands which they have bought and paid for by their sweat and blood.[7]

As we have seen, this concept of land reform via distributing Confederate lands among the emancipated blacks was included in the work plan of the Freedmen's Bureau, but the implementation of it never took place. Just the reverse. Succeeding the slain President Lincoln in office, Andrew Johnson upheld the property rights of southern landholders and in August of 1865 ordered that all confiscated lands be returned to their owners.

The Freedmen's Village at Arlington Heights, Virginia, as depicted in the May 7, 1864, issue of Harper's Weekly. *Contemporary illustrations present an idealized picture of the village, but when she lived and worked there in the 1860s, Truth found wretched "overcrowded camps" with residents living in enforced idleness. The site is now occupied by Arlington National Cemetery. Library of Congress Prints & Photographs Division/LC-USZ62-117892.*

Nonetheless, when Sojourner Truth visited Washington in 1870 and observed not only the same scene of overcrowded camps full of idle residents but additional refugees of the war still flooding in, her dismay at what to her was deepening entrenchment in dependence was answered by a resolve to work toward an alternative. As she recalled in a New York *Tribune* article,

> I made up my mind last Winter, when I saw able men and women taking dry bread from the Government to keep from starving, that I would devote myself to the cause of getting land for these people, where they can work and earn their own living in the West, where the land is so plenty.[8]

With the idea of southern land reform now quashed by the president, Truth looked to another source of land distribution for blacks: the vast government-owned and -controlled land in the trans-Mississippi West. The government was giving large amounts of land to the railroads in subsidy of their march across the continent; it was setting aside extensive land areas—even if often marginally useable land—for Native American reservations. Why not do the same for freedpersons? It would solve the contraband/refugee problem; it would cost the government less than supporting these thousands and paying the costs of the social and legal services that their continuation in the camps necessitated; and it would enable them to get off the public dole and become productive citizens, contributing economically and socially to the national well-being. Besides, it was the right thing to do. For Truth undergirded this strategy for black empowerment with a reparations rationale. Like the editor of the *Anglo-African*, Truth saw a justice issue, rather than a charity issue, in the notion of a government transfer of land to blacks. In language probably phrased by Truth's biographer Frances Titus, Truth had surveyed the imposing, monumental buildings of the capitol city, ostensibly constructed at public expense, and expressed her thoughts on the matter in this way:

> *We helped* to pay this cost. We have been a source of wealth to this republic. Our labor supplied the country with cotton, until villages and cities dotted the enterprising North for its manufacture,

and furnished employment and support for a multitude, thereby becoming a revenue to the government. . . . The overseer's horn awoke us at the dawning of day from our half-finished slumbers to pick the disgusting worm from the tobacco plant, which was an added source of wealth. Our nerves and sinews, our tears and blood, have been sacrificed on the altar of this nation's avarice. Our unpaid labor has been a stepping stone to its national success. Some of its dividends must surely be ours.[9]

The year 1816 had seen the rise of the American Colonization Society, whose mission was to set up a colony on the African continent as the resettlement ground for free-born and emancipated blacks from the United States. With $100,000 in funding from Congress in 1819, the colony of Liberia was established and received its first shipload of emigrants the following year. This colonial venture served mixed purposes. Abolitionist supporters viewed it as a viable answer to the dilemma of what to do with the blacks that they intended for their efforts to set free from slavery, since rare was the person, whether sympathetic to black freedom or not, who saw the integration of blacks with white society as acceptable. As is amply evident from statements throughout the period from both North and South, being antislavery did not necessarily mean that one was antiracism or prointegration. Proslavery forces, on the other hand, welcomed this relocation of free blacks out of the country; it was a means of eliminating both this source of agitation for emancipation and also the "problematic" modeling that free blacks represented to the enslaved as an alternative to their subjugated condition.

Sojourner Truth picked up on the "colony" idea as a useful concept for her purposes—with a modification. If the thought had been to colonize free blacks in Africa, why not "colonize" the Washington camp dwellers on government lands in the West? As she said, "This is why I am contending so in my old age. It is to teach the people that this Colony can just as well be in this country as in Liberia."[10] Truth did not seem to have in mind any nationalistic separatism for blacks. The West simply presented itself as an accessible, simple solution to a shared crisis of both blacks and the government, using a concept long in the national conversation. And a solution was needed sooner rather than later: southern forces of reaction were asserting themselves; Congress was pulling back on its commitments to Reconstruction; and the public was growing impatient with continuing efforts in behalf of freedpersons. There were voices expressing the view that enough had already been done for them.

Taking this idea of black resettlement on western land as a divine revelation, Truth set about to put her plan into effect. In the 1868 national elections, she campaigned for the presidential election of U.S. Grant, just as she had previously campaigned for Lincoln. In 1870, through the assistance of the Freedmen's Bureau director O. O. Howard and Detroit abolitionist friend Giles Stebbins, Truth was granted an audience with President Grant. It is not known whether she pressed him on the idea of western land for black resettlement, though it is likely that she raised the subject and solicited his support. Truth also visited the U.S. Senate chamber, where she was warmly received, and several legislators signed her Book of Life—her personal autograph book and scrapbook of journal articles and memorabilia. One might imagine that she also floated with this influential group her resettlement idea. However, having been told by someone that to accomplish her goal she would need to petition Congress, she had the following petition drawn up:

To the Senate and House of Representatives, in Congress assembled:

> *Whereas,* From the faithful and earnest representations of Sojourner Truth (who has personally investigated the matter), we believe that the freed colored people in and about Washington, dependent upon government for support, would be greatly benefited and might become useful citizens by being placed in a position to support themselves: We, the undersigned, therefore request your honorable body to set apart for them a portion of the public land in the West, and erect buildings thereon for the aged and infirm, and otherwise legislate so as to secure the desired results.[11]

With this petition in hand, Truth set out in late 1870 on a lecture tour to promote her idea and garner signatures.

A Northampton, Massachusetts, paper reported favorably on "the renowned Sojourner Truth's" "forcible appeals," at a town hall meeting there, that were "distinguished for native wit, eloquence, and religious pathos." The writer urged all to sign the petitions that Truth was circulating.[12] Papers from Fall River, Massachusetts, referring to her by her identity as "the colored American Sybil," reported on her lectures at two churches there in October. One writer endorsed her resettlement idea as "practical, and should be put into operation at once."[13] Not all receptions were positive, of course. A writer in a Springfield, New Jersey, paper referred to her as an "old negro mummy . . . a crazy, ignorant, repellent negress." Some in the audience of her lecture there walked out as she spoke. A correspondent to a Springfield paper, though, embarrassed by what he or she judged as the aforementioned writer's show of ignorance, spoke of "no less a personage than Sojourner Truth . . . one of the Lord's true servants . . . [who] numbers among her dearest friends the most intellectual, renowned, and gifted men and women of our land."[14]

Truth soon took advantage of two other significant opportunities to pitch the resettlement plan. She was invited to address an event called the Women's Rights Bazaar in Boston in December. In the few minutes allotted her, she argued for the equality of rights for women, which would benefit not only women but men and the whole of humanity. She then urged the idea black self-support through the provision of land in the West. Next, she was invited as one of the featured speakers for the Commemoration of the Eighth Anniversary of Negro Freedom in the United States, held January 1, 1871, at Boston's historic Tremont Temple. There, a large, standing-room-only crowd heard speeches by Dr. William Wells Brown, who, like Truth, had come out of slavery and achieved public distinction; the highly reputed Methodist Episcopal minister Rev. Gilbert Haven; the Rev. J.D. Fulton; and finally, Sojourner Truth. With her characteristic force and passion, she appealed for houses to be built in the West for the blacks languishing in Washington, so that "they can feed themselves, and they would soon be a people among you. That is my commission. Now agitate them people and put 'em there; learn 'em to read one part of the time and learn 'em to work the other part of the time." When a member of audience got up and departed, Truth, with some annoyance, said, "I'll hold awhile. Whoever is a goin' let him go. When you tell about work here, then you have to scud. [Laughter and applause.] I tell you, I can't read a book, but I can read the people. [Applause.] I speak these tings so that when you have a paper come for you to sign, you can sign it [an obvious reference to her petition]."[15]

She "spoke those tings" on several other occasions, to audiences large and small, in subsequent days, backgrounding her remarks with the narrative of her rise from slavery, segueing into her abolitionist mission, and then her new commission on behalf of the freedpersons encamped in Washington. The anchoring of her hope in a deeply con-victed personal faith was always evident. And she made her strategic aim clear: to "sends tons of paper [petitions] down to Washington for them spouters [Congresspersons] to chaw on."[16] If her speeches were plaintive and framed in incisive common sense, they could also be terse and biting. When a Philadelphia audience asked how they could help the condition of the freedpersons in Washington, she responded,

You ask me what to do for them? Do you want a poor old creeter who don't know how to read to tell edecated folks what to do? I give you the hint and you ought to know what to do. But if you don't, I can tell you. The government have given land to the rail-roads in the West; can't it do as much for these poor creeters? Let them give them land and an outset, and have teachers to learn them to read. Then they can be somebody. That's what I want. You owe it to them, because you took away from them all they earned and made them what they are. You take no interest in the colored people. . . .

You are the cause of the brutality of these poor creeters. For you're the children of those who enslaved them. That's what I want to say. I wish this hall was full to hear me. I don't want to say anything agin Anna Dickinson because she is my friend, but if she come to talk here about a woman you know nothing about, and no one knows whether there was such a woman or not [refer-ence to Miss Dickinson's lecture about Joan of Arc], you would fill this place. You want to hear nonsense. I come to tell something which you ought to listen to. You are ready to help the heathen in foreign lands, but don't care for the heathen right about you.

I want you to sign petitions to send to Washington. . . . You send these petitions, and those men in Congress will have something to spout about. I been to hear them; could make nothing out of what they said, but if they talk about the colored people I will know what they say. . . . Let the freedmen be emptied out in the West; give them land and an outset; teach them to read, and then they will be somebody. That's what I want to say.[17]

Here, as elsewhere, Truth called her audience to accountability for the conditions and the future prospects of African Americans. She challenged them to move beyond a perspective of abstract benevolence—"lets do something nice for people far away"—to fulfilling an obligation of restorative justice—reparations—for concrete wrongs committed against people right in their midst.

In February 1871, the Rev. Gilbert Haven published Truth's petition in his weekly *Zion's Herald* and conveyed to his readers his enthusiastic support. When she lectured in Boston, Haven had volunteered to help gather petition signatures and to collect the petitions sent to him from throughout Massachusetts, to forward them to Washington. In March, Horace Greeley's New York *Tribune* published the petition, and the *National Anti-Slavery Standard* published it with its hearty endorsement.

By June, Truth was back in Battle Creek. With funds accumulated from the sale of her photos at her lectures, she retired the mortgage and received the deed to the College Avenue home she had purchased from William Merritt. But she was soon off to Detroit, lodging with friend Nanette Gardner. Given Truth's advocacy for women's rights, it must have been gratifying to have Gardner write in her Book of Life that in the elections of that year, she (Gardner) had been the first woman ever to vote in a Michigan state election.

Truth was in Detroit to continue her mission to "stir up" the people to support her western land project. The Detroit *Daily Post* complimented her highly for her antislavery and women's rights work, calling her a "woman of strong religious nature, with an entirely original eloquence and humor . . . strong, clear mind, and one who, without the aid of reading or writing, is strangely susceptible to all that in thought and action is now current in the world."[18] It carried an account of her lecture and reprinted her petition. The Rev. Charles Foote, chaplain of the House of Corrections, offered to collect the signed petitions and forward them to Washington.

TO THE LAND OF EXODUS

In a letter dated December 31, 1870, Byron M. Smith, of Topeka, Kansas, invited Truth to visit that city and stay as long as she wished as a guest in his home. He even offered to pay for her transportation and travel expenses. He said that he wrote because "I know so much of you by reputation, and venerate and love so much your character" that he desired to meet her face-to-face.[19] Truth took this generous invitation from a complete stranger in the West as a divine intervention in support of her project to resettle blacks on western land. To one who had always seen each stage of her unfolding life's work as divinely initiated and undergirded, this was to her the only reasonable explanation. And so, in September of 1871, Truth boarded the train for Kansas, accompanied by her traveling mate and helper, grandson Sammy Banks. In towns en route to her destination, she took the occasion to hold meetings to publicize her project. Arriving finally in Topeka, she was welcomed by the Smiths and spoke in several venues. For the next five months, she and Sammy traveled the state, lodging with friends, old and newly made, and pressing her case for a bequest of western land for the contrabands in Washington, with a particular concern for the old and infirm among them, but generally that all there might get on a firm footing of self-sufficiency. She had initially thought that the trip to Kansas would provide the opportunity to explore potential sites for such settlement. But instead, her time was consumed in attempting to generate support for the project. Periodically in her meetings, Truth also spoke on other topics that had long been her concerns, including temperance and women's rights.

Moving on from Kansas in February 1872, Truth and Sammy continued traveling and speaking through Missouri, Iowa, Ohio, Indiana, Illinois, Michigan, and Wisconsin. Given her 70-plus years and the state of transportation in those days, such an eight-state excursion must have been grueling—even for Sammy. Traveling through the chill midwestern fall and winter seasons would have added to the physical challenge of the long journey. But Truth had put her hand to the proverbial plow and was determined not to look back. Unfortunately, in spite of her intense efforts and the enthusiastic receptions she received from audiences and media, the result was not the "ton of paper" that she had hoped to send to Washington. One person, covering so broad a landscape, perhaps could not have been expected to achieve such an outcome in such short scope of time. An organized, coordinated effort, deploying more advanced communications technologies, might have done more. Truth was a powerful, moving speaker, but she was not an organizer. Her broadly scattered, warm supporters did not coalesce into an organization, and "Twitter" was far into the future. Further, there was not unanimity among leaders sympathetic to the interests of blacks concerning Truth's idea. For instance, Frederick Douglass took the position that blacks should remain in the South and claim their rights there. Hence his paper, the *New National Era*, did not follow or encourage her efforts.

By August, Truth was in back Battle Creek, joining in the celebration of the 33rd anniversary of emancipation in the British West Indies as one of the featured speakers. And she resumed her vigorous campaigning for the reelection of U. S. Grant to the presidency, as she had done for his first election. In both cases she made it known that were his opponents to win—in this case Horace Greeley—she would move to Canada. Greeley had switched from the liberal Republican Party, the party of Lincoln and Grant, to become the Democratic nominee. When election time arrived, Truth hoped to duplicate the success of her Detroit friend Nanette Gardner in claiming the right to woman's suffrage. It was not to be. The Board of Registration declined to sign her up. When she went to the polls anyway on election day to attempt to cast a ballot, she was, again, respectfully refused.

TAKING THE CASE TO WASHINGTON

After some three years of stumping for her project, Truth decided it was time to come full circle. In the spring of 1874, with grandson Sammy at her side, she returned to Washington, to press her case with the holders of decision-making power. Her friend General O. O. Howard arranged for a speaking engagement at his church and sent a letter on her behalf to Congressman Benjamin F. Butler, another Civil War general, suggesting that some of the funds that Butler administered for housing disabled soldiers might be used for an experiment in the West along the lines that Truth was proposing. Truth had Sammy to read the letter to audiences at her speaking engagements. Butler was among the radical Republicans in Congress. He wrote the Civil Rights Act of 1871 and teamed with Senator Sumner in advancing the landmark Civil Rights Act of 1875, which outlawed racial discrimination in public accommodations. But there is no indication that Butler acted on Howard's suggestion. Nor did Congress take up Truth's proposal when she presented her petitions to that body.

Truth's project of government assistance to the destitute black dwellers in Washington's contraband camps never gained sufficient traction to come to fruition. Even many who signed her petitions did so in support of the idea but doubtful of its chances for success. Those persons who shared her belief that access to land was a key to black socioeconomic viability tended to see the South, not the West, as the region of preference. Frederick Douglass believed that blacks should take their stand for rights and equal opportunity in the South. Frances E. W. Harper, black writer and political activist who promoted many of the same causes as Truth, believed, with Truth, that education and employment were essential for black progress. But she felt that these could best come about through northern material aid and the other provisions of Reconstruction, while blacks remained in the South. At the same time, the energy for Reconstruction, the government's vehicle for a postwar restoration of the South as a functioning part of the Union, with blacks as citizen participants, was short-lived. In some areas it ended its activities as early as 1868. By 1874 the Freedmen's Bureau was defunct. And Reconstruction officially ended in 1877, with the presidential order removing federal troops from the South. In the resultant resurgence of southern political control, blacks were disenfranchised and an era of violent repression returned, including, for instance, the rise of the Ku Klux Klan. Other factors that directly or indirectly militated against Truth's western project were the lack of a national precedent for the type of social welfare intervention such as Truth proposed; the growing weariness of the white populace with the issues of the war; and the sense among many that with Emancipation enough had been done for blacks. This last position had been taken by Horace Greeley, souring the friendship that Truth had enjoyed with him.

As a revered but virtually solitary battler for the western resettlement project, it is not clear that an extended stay in Washington would ultimately have turned the tide in Truth's favor. But that would remain unclear, because not long after their arrival, Sammy became sick, having developed an aneurism on his neck, and he and Truth were forced to return to Battle Creek to see to his care. But Sammy didn't get well. Following surgery, he died in February 1875—a deep loss to Truth of one who had been more than a helper, but a precious companion. Truth herself was stricken with an ulcer on her leg. The condition became severe enough that she became bedridden and her life hung in the balance. Her condition improved under treatment from Dr. Orville Guiteau, curiously a veterinarian. Truth later recalled, "The doctors gave me up, but I got a woman doctor who got me so I could walk, but . . . my leg swelled and then I got a horse doctor who took the swelling out. . . . And I am fast improving. . . . It seems I am like a horse."[20]

While Truth was confined and convalescing, she began an important collaboration with Frances Titus, a prominent local citizen and women's suffrage activist. Titus had earlier helped Truth in her effort to relocate Washington contraband camp dwellers to Battle Creek. She now offered to publish a new edition of Truth's biography, updating the *Narrative of Sojourner Truth*, published in 1850 by Olive Gilbert. Sales of that volume through the years at her various lecturing venues had been one of Truth's main sources of financial support, combined also with sales of her *cartes de visite*. Titus underwrote the cost of publication from her personal funds. She proposed to donate the proceeds from the sale of the new 1875 volume to Truth for her to use in paying her medical expenses and the costs for Sammy's funeral, with hopes that enough additional funds would also be generated to support Truth's ongoing living expenses. The first occasion to market the book was to be the Philadelphia Centennial Exposition of 1876. Truth and Titus set out to attend the Exposition, but a recurrence of Truth's ailment forced them to abort the trip and return to Battle Creek.

Truth took her eventual recovery to a level of health wherein she could resume her activism as a sign that God had still more work for her to do, including, in her mind, a return to Washington to continue the resettlement campaign. That, however, was set aside for the time being.

NOTES

1. Frances Titus, *Narrative of Sojourner Truth; A Bondswoman of Olden Time, with a History of Her Labors and Correspondence Drawn from Her "Book of Life"* (Battle Creek, MI: Published by the author, 1878), pp. 188–89.

2. Erlene Stetson and Linda David, *Glorying in Tribulation: The Lifework of Sojourner Truth* (East Lansing: Michigan State University Press, 1994), p. 148.

3. Interview in Battle Creek *Enquirer and Evening News*, May 29, 1929, quoted in Carleton Mabee, *Sojourner Truth: Slave, Prophet, Legend* (New York: New York University Press, 1993), p. 145.

4. Rochester *Daily Democrat*, Rochester *Evening Express*, March 13, 1867, quoted in Mabee, *Sojourner Truth*, pp. 148–49.

5. Mabee, *Sojourner Truth*, p. 149.

6. "Lecture by Sojourner Truth," New York *Tribune*, November 8, 1853, p. 6.

7. Stetson and David, *Glorying in Tribulation*, p. 151.

8. Ibid., p. 153.

9. Titus, *Narrative of Sojourner Truth*, pp. 196–97.

10. Stetson and David, *Glorying in Tribulation*, p. 151.

11. Titus, *Narrative of Sojourner Truth*, p. 199.

12. Ibid., p. 200.

13. Ibid., p. 202.

14. Ibid., pp. 203–5.

15. Ibid., p. 216.

16. Ibid., p. 220.

17. Ibid., p. 226.

18. Ibid, p. 237.

19. Ibid., p. 240.

20. Martin L. Ashley, "Frances Titus: Sojourner's 'Trusted Scribe,'" *Heritage Battle Creek, A Journal of Local History* 8 (Fall 1997), http://www.sojournertruth.org/Library/Archive/Titus-TrustedScribe.htm.

Chapter 9

SAME SONG,
NEW VERSES

In 1877, Truth and Titus set out again on a speaking tour. With Truth's age and health presenting increasing challenges for travel, Titus took up grandson Sammy's role as traveling aide, serving also as Truth's business manager and the one who handled her correspondence. As they traveled through western Michigan, they sold the new biography and Truth's *cartes de visite*. Truth's main subject for these lectures was temperance, primarily associated in the 19th-century United States with the movement to curtail the consumption of alcoholic beverages. The movement was largely advanced by women, who credited the abuse of alcohol with domestic violence, husbands' dissipation of family financial resources, and even broader destructive consequences for society. It was an issue in both Europe and the United States, generating widespread activist energy, on a level with the abolition and women's rights movements. Temperance societies sprang up around the nation. Clergy advanced the movement from the pulpit, and some churches came to have periodic "Temperance Sundays" as part of their Sunday School program. The movement, under groups such as Frances Willard's Woman's Christian Temperance Union (WCTU), became increasingly assertive and sought to implement its aims through national legislation.

During her days of enslavement, Sojourner Truth imbibed and enjoyed alcoholic beverages. They were a part of the reward and celebration provisions of owners to their chattel workers, especially on holidays. Her views on alcohol may have changed, however, when she affiliated with Methodism, whose denominations, black and white, took clear stands for temperance. The leaders of the Matthias Kingdom, which Truth joined in New York, opposed consumption of alcohol. And when she took up residence in the Northampton community, she fully embraced temperance, it being among the deep commitments held by the noted residents and visitors to that place, including William Lloyd Garrison. In addition, Truth's close association with women's rights groups may have further formed her views on this subject. The home was understood, in the thinking of the times, as the appropriate "sphere" of women's activities. Because women saw the immoderate consumption of alcohol as a threat to the financial and relational stability of the home, they took it as within their prerogatives to speak out for temperance, as a defense of the home. Thus, a door was opened for a public voice for women, since it fit in the larger context of their designated domestic sphere responsibilities. In time, this logic extended to having a public say on the subject, that is, a vote. And if a vote was justified here, why not on other, wider social issues?

By the 1870s, Truth became an advocate for temperance, as she had earlier been for women's rights generally. She frequently lectured on it or included it as a point in her lectures for other causes. Speaking before the Michigan state legislature in June 1881, she offered her particular take on temperance and how to address it:

> I should like to see you make a law that would hang whiskey out of the United States, for I believe that it is at the bottom of a great many crimes. In a great many cases it is not the man that murders, but the whiskey. There is one trouble about this temperance work. You get a man to sign the [temperance] pledge and that is all there is of it, when you ought to get him to work, and carry food and clothing to his poor starving wife and children. Treat them as human beings should be treated and fewer temperance converts would backslide.[1]

Truth sold her cartes de visite *for many years in order to help meet her living expenses. Library of Congress Prints & Photographs Division/LC-DIG-ppmsca-08978.*

Frances Willard's WCTU published the claim that Truth "has probably delivered more temperance addresses than any other person living."[2]

"FREED FROM THE FILTHY WEED"

While temperance was typically associated with abstinence from alcohol, moderation or abstinence relative to other practices was also in its purview. As with drinking, Truth had been a smoker since her youth. And again, as with drinking, Truth was probably led to abstinence, in principle and in practice, by the associations she came to make. Smoking was denounced as a health-destroying, filthy waste of money by women's groups, as well as by the religious groups among whom Truth had friendships and intimate interaction throughout her adult years, such as the Quakers, Spiritualists, and the Seventh Day Adventists. They often designated drinking and smoking as twin destructive evils.

Beyond pressure from her associates, smoking was also a practical problem in Truth's social mission. For it was a somewhat tricky proposition for her to advocate responsible spending to struggling blacks when she herself was spending from her limited resources on a nonessential indulgence like smoking. It was equally problematic to advocate abstinence from one unhealthy substance, alcohol, when she was regularly indulging in another, tobacco.

Truth tried several times over the years to give up smoking. Perhaps the turning point came for her when she was challenged on the basis of her loyalty to her religious convictions, the proving ground of all of her work. The following story was printed in the March 7, 1868, edition of the Coldwater, Michigan, *Republican:*

SOJOURNER TRUTH

This old colored woman, now living in Michigan, recently visited Milton, Wisconsin, where she was the guest of a Mr. [Joseph] Goodrich, who was an out-and-out temperance man, and a noted hater of tobacco. One morning she was puffing away with a long pipe in her mouth when her host, Mr. Goodrich, approached her, and commenced conversation with the following interrogatory.

"Aunt Sojourner, do you think you are a Christian?"

"Yes, Brudder Goodrich, I speck I am."

"Aunt Sojourner, do you believe in the bible?"

"Yes, Brudder Goodrich, I bleeve the scripters, though I can't read 'em, as you can."

"Aunt Sojourner, do you know that there is a passage in the scriptures which declares that nothing unclean shall inherit the kingdom of heaven?"

"Yes, Brudder Goodrich, I have heard tell of it."

"Aunt Sojourner, do you believe it?"

"Yes, Brudder Goodrich, I bleeve it?"

"Well, Aunt Sojourner, you smoke, and you cannot enter the kingdom of heaven, because there is nothing so unclean as the breath of a smoker. What do you say to that?"

"Why, Brudder Goodrich, I speck to leave my breff behind me when I go to heaven."[3]

One might "speck" Goodrich thought he had her, but characteristic of Truth's cagey repartee, she finessed her way out. Or did she? Did it prick a nerve of religious conviction that contributed toward a faith response? Was a seed planted in this interchange that germinated into a change of heart and mind as it continued to be nurtured by her anti-smoking associates? On January 18, 1869, Truth sent this letter to her Rochester friend Amy Post:

> I want you to let it be known that it was of my own will and de-sire to quit smoking. It was the Spirit that spoke to me to give up tobacco, and I long had been wishing to do so, but could not, and I prayed to God that he would make me feel the necessity to give it up, and he did and I have had no taste or appetite to take it . again. Tell Miss Coleman [Lucy Colman] that [it] was all of my own power or the power that God gave me to give up tobacco, & now my great prayer is that all who smoke may have the Spirit that spoke to me to work in them to destroy the desire for tobacco.[4]

In later years, Truth used the Goodrich argument in her own temperance appeals against smoking.

EXODUS LAND REDUX

The ending of Reconstruction, with its resultant antiblack violence, sexual abuse of black women, and black disenfranchisement, combined with crop failures and generally discouraging prospects for black advancement, led many black southerners to consider movement out of the South. Kansas had a particular appeal for blacks of this mind, since it was the place in which the legendary John Brown had fought against slavery, and since it had, in fact, been admitted to the Union in January 1861, as a free state. Thus, the first big wave of southern black emigration, which came to be known as the Colored Exodus, chose Kansas as its primary destination. Within the first few months of 1879, some 50,000 blacks had moved North.

The Convention of Louisiana Negroes, meeting in April of 1879, heartily approved of the move. A large number of those in this first of many waves of emigration had come from that state. Henry Adams, a driving force in the move, testified before Congress that a committee organized to explore options for southern black emigration initially looked to find the best places in the South for relocation. But after visits to each region, the conclusion was that no place in the South offered a viable option. Violence, including blatant murder; political repression; extortion of wages; and other hostile conditions were pervasive. "Every State in the South had got into the hands of the very men that held us slaves." Appeals to Congress and to both Presidents Grant and Hayes had brought no relief. So emigration was chosen because, said Adams, testifying at a hearing of a U.S. Senate committee investigating the movement,

> [I]n my judgment, and from what information I have received, and what I have seen with my own eyes—it is because the largest majority of the people, of the white people, that held us as slaves treats our people so bad in many respects that it is impossible for us to stand it. . . . [O]ur people most as well be slaves as to be free."

Similar testimony was offered to the hearing by other southern blacks who were knowledgeable about the emigration.[5]

At a meeting of the National Conference of Colored Men of the United States, held in Nashville, Tennessee, in May of 1879, a letter read from the Charleston, South Carolina, Colored Western Emigration Society asked, "What is mere freedom to man without civil and political rights?" Stating that blacks have "willing hands" and "strong arms," the letter "appeal[ed] to the good people of the country to aid us in changing the place of our abode to the free States and Territories."[6] The Committee on Address of the conference spoke approvingly of emigration: "The disposition to leave the communities in which they feel insecure, is an evidence of a healthy growth in manly independence, and should receive the commendation and support of all philanthropists."[7] A resolution introduced by W. H. Councill of Alabama affirmed emigration in principle, as a legitimate option, while questioning whether it was premature and cautioning that it should not be done en masse, nor without due consideration as to whether it would better the condition of those undertaking it.

Frederick Douglass, on the other hand, addressing the American Social Science Association in September 1879, took the position that while the movement of emigration put to the lie the claim that blacks did not have the strength of moral character to take action for their rights, and while it would, in fact, address many of the needs of a people transitioning from slavery to free citizenship, nonetheless, blacks should not concede their rights by abandoning the contest in the South. Douglass viewed this as

> a premature, disheartening surrender, since it would make free-dom and free institutions depend upon migration rather than protection; by flight rather than by right. . . . It leaves the whole question of equal rights on the soil of the South open and still to be settled . . . it is a confession of the utter impracticability of equal rights and equal protection in any State, where those rights may be struck down by violence.

Thus, in evocative metaphorical characterization, Douglass declared that the "Exodus is medicine, not food."[8]

For Sojourner Truth, the Exodus, this mass movement of belea-guered southern blacks to the West, was a vindication of the vision to which she had dedicated her energies and expended her resources, in-cluding, perhaps, her health, in years of a petition drive. Upon learn-ing of it, Truth revised and updated her Civil War song lyrics to herald this new manifestation of what, to her eyes, was God's plan moving forward:

> The word it has been spoken; the message has been sent;
> The prison doors have opened, and out the prisoners went.
> To join the sable army of African descent, for God is marching on.[9]

In August of 1879, Truth and companion/ colaborer Frances Titus set out for Kansas to see her dream playing out and, as needed, to assist the "Exodusters" in their resettlement. Stopping by Chicago en route, Truth spoke at the Langley Avenue Methodist Church. As reported in a local paper, Truth expressed her belief that

> The movement means the regeneration, temporally and spiritu-ally, of the American colored race, and I always knew the Lord

Frances Titus (1816–1894). Titus, a Quaker, was Truth's friend and traveling companion and the editor of the 1870s and 1880s versions of the Narrative of Sojourner Truth. *Courtesy of the Willard Library, Battle Creek, Michigan.*

would find some way. . . . There will be, chile, a great glory come out of that. . . . The colored people is going to be a people. Do you think God has had them robbed and scourged them all the days of their life for nothing."[10]

Arriving in Kansas in September, Truth and Titus volunteered with the Kansas Freedmen's Relief Association. Like the contrabands in the Washington camps, the Kansas Exodusters had broad needs for food, shelter, and employment assistance, which was the reason for the organization of the Relief Association. Truth and Titus worked alongside Laura Haviland and Elizabeth Comstock, Quaker women from Michigan, also there to serve the needs of the migrants. Haviland, like Titus, had previously cooperated with Truth in relief efforts on behalf of the Washington contrabands. It was Haviland who was with Truth in the encounter with the Washington transportation system that resulted in Truth's successful lawsuit.

In the Kansas effort, Haviland and Compton became, in effect, the managers of the Relief Association program. Truth did what she had always done most effectively, and what her advancing age and declining state of health would most allow, namely, speaking on behalf of the cause. She spoke encouragement and motivation to the settlers in their temporary barracks. She spoke in black and white churches, generating popular support for the reception of continuing emigrants, as well as for material aid for their needs. She and Titus did travel through areas of the state delivering wagon loads of provisions that had been donated. But the direct service was primarily done by others, under the direction of Haviland and Compton. Compton reported appreciatively of the good work being accomplished through Truth's labors. And Truth pronounced the whole effort to be "God directed."[11]

Having originally planned to stay for a month, Truth and Titus got caught up in the needs of the work and, perhaps, in the satisfaction of being part of a historically momentous event. So they extended their stay through early December, when Truth, Titus, and Haviland left Kansas to continue promoting the relief and resettlement work in other states. For instance, in Streator, Illinois, and in Chicago, they spoke on behalf of the cause and collected donations to be sent back to Kansas.

By mid-January 1880, Truth was back in her home in Battle Creek. She must certainly have continued to monitor the progress of the Kansas Exodus experience, as successive waves of migrants flowed in and took their places among the even larger number of whites, including many European emigrants, who were coming to this space to seek their fortunes. While she did not take credit for the Exodus, she did see in it God doing what she had prayed for for years. Where she had looked to Western land as a resettlement place for destitute, dependent refugees in Washington, the Exodusters were from the South. Nor were her visions of government assistance for resettlement, nor blacks becoming significant landowners, realized in this movement. Nonetheless, the Exodus to Kansas was, in a real way, a fulfillment, in actuality and in potential, of what Truth had envisioned for blacks: the chance to establish for themselves a ground of viable self-sufficiency; the chance to develop habits of industry; the chance to gain education and nurture the personal characteristics of responsible, loyal citizens—to become "a people." And she was confident that her God would bring it about.

NOTES

1. Mary G. Butler, ed., *On Temperance, in The Words Of Truth*, http://www.sojournertruth.org/Library/Speeches/Default.htm.

2. Chicago *Signal*, September 8, 1881, quoted in Carleton Mabee, *Sojourner Truth: Slave, Prophet, Legend* (New York: New York University Press, 1993), p. 198.

3. "Varieties," National Library of New Zealand, Paperspast, Star, Issue 80, August 15, 1868, p. 3, http://paperspast.natlib.govt.nz/cgi-bin/paperspast?a=d&cl=search&d=WCT18680829.2.23&srpos=13&e=—10—11—on—2%22strange+creature%22-article.

4. Quoted in Mabee, *Sojourner Truth*, p. 197.

5. Cited material taken from *Senate Report 693*, 46th Congress, 2nd Session, part 2, pp. 101–11, reprinted in Herbert Aptheker, *A Documentary History of the Negro People in the United States*, vol. 2 (New York: Citadel Press, 1970), pp. 720–21.

6. Taken from "Proceedings of the National Conference of Colored Men of the United States," held in the State Capitol at Nashville, TN, May 6–9, 1879, reprinted in Aptheker, *A Documentary History*, p. 724.

7. Ibid.

8. Taken from "Addresses Delivered before the American Social Science Association," September, 12, 1879, and published in the *Journal of Social Science* (Boston, May, 1880), reprinted in Aptheker, *A Documentary History*, pp. 724–26.

9. Quoted in Erlene Stetson and Linda David, *Glorying in Tribulation: The Lifework of Sojourner Truth* (East Lansing: Michigan State University Press, 1994), p. 154.

10. "Sojourner Truth," Chicago *Inter Ocean*, August 13, 1879, p. 3.

11. Mabee, *Sojourner Truth*, p. 166.

Chapter 10

"SOMETHING REMAINS FOR ME TO DO"

Sojourner Truth, nee Isabella Bomefree, was born into a world that presumed the dominance of men in essentially all aspects of communal life. The presumption was based in the prior assumption of the superior capabilities of men in rational thought, which, in the Age of Enlightenment, took precedence over intuition, emotion, even revelation, in the management of society. It was also based in the assumed and more objectively verifiable superior physical power of men generally, in a time before technology diminished, even nullified, the value of might and physical prowess in negotiating and securing the processes that sustained viable communal life. But just as critically, the presumption of male dominance and superior privileging over women was based in the assumption of a superior fundamental worth of men over women, congruent with assumptions of the superior fundamental worth of certain racial/ethnic groups over others, of adults over minors, and of certain religious and cultural traditions over others. These assumptions had been accorded validation by the theological and philosophical tenets that stood behind the laws, customs, thought processes, and other ruling structures of society. They were taken as unchallengeable givens.

Sojourner Truth emerged into womanhood as a person with a mind-set averse to subjection to the givens of society, including those regarding gender. She possessed a strong sense of selfhood, as a person whose gender happened to be female and whose integrity she would not consent to be violated. Her living circumstances as an enslaved member of a denigrated class of persons did not allow her the opportunity to have inculcated into her the Victorian ideal of the female as fragile and vulnerable, pedestaled above the rough-and-tumble fray of the world, and retiring in the face of men. Thus, she could break all convention by presuming as a woman, and a black woman at that, to bring a lawsuit against a white man—more than once in her lifetime.

But further than this assertion of her gendered selfhood, Sojourner Truth asserted that there were positive, distinct capabilities that women *as women* had to offer the human enterprise, ones that enabled them both to function on a par with men and also, even, to correctively counterbalance the inadequate social performance of men. Hence, she argued using the analogy that if women's intellect was only at the level of a pint, compared to men's quart, then her pint was equal in actual practice to that quart. She argued that though the preeminence of men was said to be rooted in Jesus Christ being a male, that that male Christ was born of a *woman*. And if one woman, Eve, was powerful enough single-handedly to turn the world upside down, then the collective body of woman in her day surely was equally capable of turning it back right side up.[1]

Throughout her years of speaking for women's rights, Truth pressed this case yet further, contending that women possessed the wisdom, the force, and the human sensitivity to undo the social/political mess that men had made of things in the world. Women's ascension into leadership would achieve what men had thus far shown themselves to be incapable of accomplishing. As women could clean up houses made messy by men, they could clean up governmental processes of which men had made a mess. Thus, women should have access to becoming lawyers, judges, jurors, and members of Congress. In her words, "As men have been endeavoring for years to govern alone, and have not yet succeeded in perfecting any system, it is about time women should take the matter in hand."[2] Truth's assertion that women in governmental leadership would end warfare finds interesting parallel in the call of Truth's contemporary, Julia Ward Howe, for women to meet in convention to find a pathway to replacing warfare with peace in human relationships. Howe's 1870 Proclamation of a Mother's Day for Peace read, in part,

Arise then . . . women of this day!
Arise, all women who have hearts!
Whether your baptism be of water or of tears!
Say firmly:
"We will not have questions answered by irrelevant agencies,
Our husbands will not come to us, reeking with carnage,
For caresses and applause.
Our sons shall not be taken from us to unlearn
All that we have been able to teach them of charity, mercy and patience.
We, the women of one country,
Will be too tender of those of another country
To allow our sons to be trained to injure theirs.
As men have often forsaken the plough and the anvil
At the summons of war,
Let women now leave all that may be left of home
For a great and earnest day of counsel. . . .
In the name of womanhood and humanity, I earnestly ask
That a general congress of women without limit of nationality,
May be appointed and held at someplace deemed most convenient
And the earliest period consistent with its objects,
To promote the alliance of the different nationalities,
The amicable settlement of international questions,
The great and general interests of peace.[3]

FOR THE RIGHTS OF WOMEN

In Sojourner Truth's first experience of living in an intentional community, the Matthias Kingdom in New York, leaders Pierson and Matthias placed women in subordinate status and forbade them to take leadership roles. Truth accommodated herself to that model. But beginning in 1844, in the Northampton Association, Truth encountered persons who advocated both for abolition and for the rights of women. Her own natural inclination to asserting her agency as a female was thus given room for expression and encouragement, just as was her passion for righting the wrongs of slavery, so wrenchingly experienced in her own life. These two became interwoven themes as she went forth on her faith-based mission of social justice.

Women's rights was not an abstract concern. By law and custom, there were unequal rights in the home; restrictions on what jobs women could hold outside the home; unequal pay for doing the same work as men; limitations on women's ability to inherit property, to control their income, to share with their spouses in the control of their children, and even to control the sanctity and use of their own bodies. In her dual identity as an enslaved woman, Truth had witnessed how each of these played out as deep concerns for women, even within relationships among the enslaved.

At the historic Ohio Women's Rights Convention of 1851, Truth began marking some of the themes of her argument for women's rights and debunking the premises by which they were being withheld. For instance, if citizen's rights and privileges accrued to men based on their ability to do the work that sustained society, she, as a woman, could match the work production of men, so should not she receive those rights—she and all other women who could so prove themselves? But the "exceptionalism" of some women was not the issue; it was whether women as a class should be summarily excluded from their rightful due as citizens based on questionable eligibility standards. In the course of her extemporaneous remarks to the convention, Truth rebutted several other claims of male antagonists to women's rights based on the alleged incapacity or unfitness of women to exercise the full rights accorded to men.

At the Broadway Temple women's rights convention of 1853, Truth administered a slashing rebuke to the men present whose uncouth, disruptive behavior garnered for the meeting the name "Mob Convention." But she also made there the self-assured declaration that the achievement of women's rights was unstoppable; it was going to come about in spite of whatever efforts to the contrary its opponents might put forth. This defiant assertiveness was another face of Truth's attitude toward women's achievement of their rights. On the one hand, she was confident that there was an inevitability to this aspect of equity in human social relationships. On the other hand, she somewhat impatiently admonished women not to sit back and timidly request of men their rights or sheepishly wait for men to concede them their due. Rather, if they wanted rights, they should step forth and take them. Her own life was an example for this, for in claiming her freedom from master Dumont and in reclaiming her son Peter from unlawful removal into slavery, Truth had defied custom and gender-role definition and asserted what she believed to be her rights. She would later do the same, equally defiantly and boldly, in challenging segregation in the public transportation system of Washington, D.C.

In 1866, while working to resettle the freedpersons encamped around Washington, Truth and African American poet Frances Ellen Watkins Harper spoke on behalf of rights for blacks and for women at meetings in New York and Boston. Then, in May of 1867, Truth traveled again to New York City, at the invitation of Susan B. Anthony and Elizabeth Cady Stanton, to speak at the First Annual Meeting of the American Equal Rights Association. She spent a week there as a guest in Stanton's home. Anthony and Stanton, like Truth, had long been strong voices for the abolition of slavery, while also advancing the cause of rights for women. They had worked together around these dual aims. With the Civil War now over and emancipation accomplished, Anthony and Stanton believed it was time to prioritize women's concerns. Congress had passed the Thirteenth Amendment to the Constitution, outlawing slavery. It was now considering the Fourteenth Amendment, which would expand the definition of "citizen" and guarantee "equal protection" for all citizens in the enjoyment of their rights and freedom. Congress was also considering a Fifteenth Amendment, which would prohibit the denial of suffrage, the right to vote, based on "race, color, or previous condition of servitude." The crucial question for women's suffragists was whether these amendments would include or exclude women, black or white, when it came to the right to vote.

Stanton, Truth, Anthony, and other women's suffragists, had argued that the vote for blacks and for women must not be uncoupled. In principle, citizenship and its rights belonged to both. Prominent male abolition advocates, such as Frederick Douglass and William Lloyd Garrison, had spoken out for women's rights. But the organizers of the convention were raising some strategic issues, rooted in their concerns about prevailing patterns of gender relationships. Believing the resistance of men as men to women voting was as strong as, if not stronger than, white resistance to blacks voting, Stanton wanted to make the point to the Equal Rights Convention that to give black men the vote and not women would just be stacking a male deck against women. Truth agreed that women should be given voting rights with men. She was particularly concerned about the implications of this within the black community, because her experience was that black men had picked up their model of gender relationships from their slave masters and tended to treat black women in the same domineering and abusive ways as white men did. Thus, black women needed the vote for their own protection.

Truth understood her involvement in the women's rights issue, as with all her other justice activities, to be expressions of her God-directed mission. She told the convention that at her age, "it is about time for me to be going." But, "I suppose I am kept here because something remains for me to do; I suppose I am yet to help break the chain." Her lectures over the two days of the convention, among the few full-length accounts of her many public addresses, offer the range of her arguments on the subject and reflect the insightful and incisive character of her thought. They are worth extended excerpts here.

> My friends, I am rejoiced that you are glad, but I don't know how you will feel when I get through. I come from another field—the country of the slave. They have got their liberty—so much good luck to have slavery partly destroyed; not entirely. I want it root and branch destroyed. Then we will all be free indeed. I feel that if I have to answer for the deeds done in my body just as much as a man,[4] I have a right to have just as much as a man. There is a great stir about colored men getting their rights, but not a word about the colored women; and if colored men get their rights, and not colored women theirs, you see the colored men will be masters over the colored women, and it will be just as bad as it was before. So I am for keeping the thing going while things are stirring; because if we wait till it is still, it will take a great while to get it going again.[5]

Truth first raises a common note in her lectures on women's rights: equity. While she later speaks of equal pay for equal work by women of all ethnic groups, she here casts the matter in more cosmic terms: equal accountability before God for "deeds done in the body" requires equal opportunity to control her body and its productions. She then notes that the buzz of the convention has not included any recognition of the particular concerns of black women, either because their concerns have been ignored or lumped with those of middle-class white women, as though they were the same. She is here also pointing out the reality of the triple, interlocking oppressions of black women—gender, race, and class—and the necessity of addressing the three as a whole. Other than Truth, few among 19th-century reformers did so. Then, in using the metaphor of acting "while things are stirring," Truth was speaking from her biblical frame of reference. The Christian New Testament speaks of the Pool of Bethesda in Jerusalem, around which persons with various infirmities gathered, because, as the belief went, at certain times an angel would stir up the waters of the pool, and the first one to enter while the waters were stirring received healing of their condition. Thus it was critical to act at the opportune moment—"while things are stirring"—since one could not predict when such an opportunity would come again. Speaking on the second day of the convention, Truth made an even more direct application of this biblical model. She said,

> I am glad to see that men are getting their rights, but I want women to get theirs, and while the water is stirring I will step into the pool. Now that there is a great stir about colored men getting their rights, it is time for women to step in and have theirs.[6]

Truth restated the central concern of the convention, but in a way that linked men's social redemption with that of women.

> Men have got their rights, and women has not got their rights. That is the trouble. When women gets her rights man will be right. How beautiful that will be. Then it will be peace on earth and goodwill to men. But it cannot be that until it be right.[7]

Truth then spoke to the "fitness" of women to vote or be in public leadership:

> [I]t was said to me some time ago that "a woman was not fit to have any rule. Do you want women to rule? They ain't fit. Don't you know that a woman had seven devils in her, and do you suppose that a man should put her to rule in the government." "Seven devils is of no account," said I, "just behold, the man had a legion." They never thought about that. A man had a legion and the devils didn't know where to go. That was the trouble. They asked if they might get among the swine; they thought it was about as good a place as where they came from. Why didn't the devils ask to go among the sheep? But no. But that may have been selfish of the devils and certainly a man has a little touch of that selfishness that don't want to give the women their right.

Truth pointed out to the male advancers of the "fitness" argument that scripture was not on their side. If demon possession was a disqualifier, then *men* had a problem, because if the woman in the scriptural story in question, Mary Magdalene, had a few demons, the man, the "Gerasene demoniac," had a legion of them. Furthermore, the scriptures praise that woman's faithfulness and she travels with Jesus, whereas the man, who asks to travel with Jesus, is told to go home. For Truth, the fitness argument is settled by this and similar scriptural affirmations of women while men are critiqued. And so, she concludes, "The truth will reign triumphant."

In the evening of the second day of the convention, Truth reflected, in striking, poignant terms, on her life in the rights struggle, in the context of recent national events and the urgency of present possibilities:

> I have lived on through all that has taken place these forty years in the anti-slavery cause, and I have plead with all the force I had that the day might come that the colored people might own their soul and body. Well, the day has come, although it came through blood. It makes no difference how it came—it did come. I am sorry it came in that way. We are now trying for liberty that requires no blood—that women shall have their rights—not rights

from you [men.] Give them what belongs to them; they ask it kindly, too. I ask it kindly. Now I want it done very quick. It can be done in a few years.[8]

Just as the rights of blacks, tragically achieved through war, were not human bequests but were "endowed by the Creator," so, also, are the rights of women their natural heritage; they "belong to them" and should be opened up as soon as legislatively feasible—presumably her reference to "in a few years." Encouraging women, thus, to claim what is already theirs, she says,

I know that it is hard for [men,] who has held the reins for so long to give up; it cuts like a knife. It will feel all the better when it closes up again. . . . [So] be strong women! Blush not! Tremble not! I know men will get up and brat, brat, brat, brat about something which does not amount to anything except talk. We want to carry the point to one particular thing, and that is women's rights, for nobody has any business with a right that belongs to her. I can make use of my own right. I want the same use of the same right. Do you want it? Then get it. If men had not taken something that did not belong to them they would not fear. But they tremble! They dodge! We will have nothing owned by anybody.

She reminded her hearers that "Men speak great lies" and that even good men are prone to say the right things in discussion and then take it half back. So, women "must make a little allowance," but also "keep a good faith and a good courage."[9]

WHICH WAY TO RIGHTS?

Sojourner Truth's lectures to the Equal Rights Convention were well-received by the audiences and commended by the press. Anthony, Stanton, and the other organizers undoubtedly were pleased—as far as her comments went. But there was an undercurrent of discontent that rose to the surface, challenging the unity and straining the relationships of long-time cohorts in the social justice struggle. The dispossession and marginalization of both blacks and women in the pre–Civil

War period made abolition and women's rights very congenial justice subjects, easily drawing a Frederick Douglass and a Susan B. Anthony to the same platform, supporting each other's primary cause, indeed, seeing them as different dimensions of the same cause. With the war over and the legislative processes moving to elevate blacks to full citizens' rights, some asked if not the same should happen, equally, for women, their colaborers for justice.

In the time following the northern success in the war and the resultant ending of slavery, many abolitionists declared that "this hour belongs to the Negro." Emancipation alone was not sufficient. Continuing "rebel" sentiment in the South, the resurgence of antiblack violence, and the efforts of southern Democrats to reassert their repressive control over southern blacks meant that laws and protections needed to be put into place to preserve the war's potential positive outcomes. This was seemingly behind Truth's statement at the convention that slavery was "partly destroyed; not entirely;" that she wanted it "root and branch destroyed." For some persons with these concerns, the focus was upon the black male, incorporating them into the universal manhood suffrage that had come to be the practice in the land. Certainly some held the prevailing position that the vote was properly for men. Others, though, saw a critical strategic issue at stake, relative to racial protection: if the vote were extended to all women, then southern women could vote and would thus swell the ranks of those who would likely vote for the overthrow of the gains of the war and emancipation.

Women's suffragists who had been supporters of abolition became increasingly aggravated by this turn of thought. One of the chief reasons for inviting Truth to the 1869 Equal Rights Convention was to add the weight of her name and speaking influence to the cause of joint elevation of blacks and women. They were particularly incensed that the proposed language of the Fourteenth Amendment would insert, for the first time, the word "male" into the Constitution, making gender a qualification for voting. With the exception of this problematic provision, the Fourteenth Amendment extended broad protections of the rights of black men and women. It therefore drew support among abolitionists and some women's rights advocates. But others saw it as a setback to women, and its supporters as betrayers of what had been a common agenda. Increasingly, suffragists of this persuasion began lobbying against the passage of this amendment, as well as the subsequently proposed Fifteenth Amendment, which specifically extended the vote to all males, regardless of "race, color, or previous condition of servitude."

The Equal Rights Convention had been established to push for the mutual rise to full citizenship rights of women and blacks. But the controversy over the Fourteenth and Fifteenth Amendments became a source of divisive tension. Susan B. Anthony and Elizabeth Cady Stanton, key promoters of the convention, took an ever firmer position in favor of full rights for blacks coming only in tandem with full rights for women. They feared, in the terms of Truth's lecture metaphor, that if women did not "step in" while the waters of suffrage reform were stirring, it would be extremely difficult to open the opportunity again any time soon. Stanton's rhetoric on the subject became increasingly harsh, nativist, even racialist. Already in 1865 she had argued the point that women had fought long for black liberation, putting their own liberation on the back burner, but now that blacks were free, "it becomes a serious question whether we had better stand aside and see 'Sambo' walk into the kingdom first."[10] By the January 1869, meeting of the Equal Rights Association, an even more embittered Stanton railed against the immigrant influx into the United States of persons from China, Germany, England, Ireland, and Africa. She opposed the intent of the Fifteenth Amendment to enfranchise all male citizens, thus allowing "Patrick and Sambo and Hans and Tung [Irish, blacks, Germans, and Chinese] to legislate for white women. She wondered aloud to the audience how white male politicians could stoop to 'make their wives and mothers the political inferiors of unlettered and unwashed ditch-diggers, bootblacks, butchers, and barbers, fresh from the slave plantations of the South, and the effete civilizations of the Old World.'"[11]

In another place she protested "the enfranchisement of another man of any race or clime until the daughters of Jefferson, Hancock, and Adams are crowned with their rights."[12] Frederick Douglass, present at the meeting, challenged Stanton on her use of racially stereotypical language and the privileging of the daughters of white "founding fathers" over other women. He also rejected Anthony's suggestion that if suffrage could not be extended to all, it should be given to the "most intelligent" and educated first, an idea that clearly would privilege middle- to upper-class whites.

By this meeting, also, Anthony and Stanton had seen the ratification of the Fourteenth Amendment and the willingness of former abolitionist colleagues to push for further legal protections for blacks, via solidifying black male suffrage, as opposed to coupling that irrevocably to seeking universal women's suffrage. So Anthony and Stanton had been forming alliances with antiblack Democrats who agreed to support granting the vote to all women. And following the 1869 meeting, the Equal Rights Association was split, with Anthony and Stanton organizing the National Woman Suffrage Association (NWSA), with a journal, *The Revolution,* supported by racialist Democrat George Francis Train. Lucy Stone, Henry Blackwell, Thomas Wentworth Higginson, and Julia Ward Howe formed the American Woman Suffrage Association (AWSA), dedicated to the ratification of the Fifteenth Amendment and to a campaign for a new amendment giving the vote to women.

In her lectures at the 1867 Equal Rights Association, Sojourner Truth had steered a middle ground between the two conflicted approaches to universal rights. Her lectures had given insight and encouragement to both sides. She was not present for the 1869 meeting to witness or participate in the clashes that previewed its split. Ultimately she chose to align with the American Woman Suffrage Association. And in 1870, she joined in celebration of the ratification that year of the Fifteenth Amendment, thereby implying her support for that measure that protected the right of black men to vote.

Truth's investment in rights for women was deep and genuine, and she continued to speak at meetings and conventions gathered for that purpose. But by this time she had become energized around her effort to secure a government grant of land in the West for the resettlement of the freedpersons in the Washington camps. So she tended to use her lectures and remarks at subsequent gatherings primarily to advance that cause, though still making valuable contributions to the thrust to honor the rights of women, whom she deemed the "mothers of creation."

NOTES

1. See The Sojourner Truth Institute, http://www.sojournertruth. org/Library/Archive/LibyanSibyl.htm; Frances Titus, *Narrative of Sojourner Truth; A Bondswoman of Olden Time, with a History of Her Labors and Correspondence Drawn from Her "Book of Life"* (Battle Creek, MI: Published by the author, 1878), p. 135.

2. Carleton Mabee, *Sojourner Truth: Slave, Prophet, Legend* (New York: New York University Press, 1993), p. 176.

3. See http://womenshistory.about.com/od/howejwriting/a/moth ers_day.htm; Titus, *Narrative of Sojourner Truth*, p. 243.

4. Reference to St. Paul's statements about the Last Judgment in II Corinthians 5:10 of the Christian New Testament.

5. Janey Weinhold Montgomery, *A Comparative Analysis of Two Negro Women Orators—Sojourner Truth and Frances E. Watkins Harper* (Hays: Fort Hays Kansas State College, 1968), p. 98.

6. Ibid., p. 99.

7. Manning Marable, *Freedom on My Mind* (New York: Columbia University Press, 2003), p. 6.

8. Montgomery, *A Comparative Analysis*, p. 100.

9. Ibid., p. 99; Suzanne Pullon Fitch and Roseann M. Mandziuk, *Sojourner Truth As Orator* (Westport, CT: Greenwood Press, 1997), pp. 128–29.

10. Quoted in Erlene Stetson and Linda David, *Glorying in Tribulation: The Lifework of Sojourner Truth* (East Lansing: Michigan State University Press, 1994), p. 166.

11. J. H. Baker, ed., *Votes for Women: The Struggle for Suffrage Revisited* (Oxford: Oxford University Press, 2002), p. 51.

12. Quoted in A. A. Lunsford, *Reclaiming Rhetorica: Women in the Rhetorical Tradition* (Pittsburgh: University of Pittsburgh Press, 1995), p. 240.

Chapter 11

"AIN'T GOT TIME TO DIE": STILL WORKING IN THE SUNSET

When Harriet Beecher Stowe published her 1863 *Libyan Sybil* article, recounting her meeting with Sojourner Truth, she indicated to her readers wistfully that the woman who had made such an impression on her had passed from this life. But this report of Truth's death was "greatly exaggerated" (as Mark Twain had quipped about rumors of his own death). In her sixties, Truth did begin to feel the weight of her years and thought of settling down to a less active schedule. And on more than one occasion, health challenges confined her to bed and even brought her seemingly to the point of death. But always she sprang back; always her sense of mission, of being under assignment from her God to address the critical justice needs of the world, pulled her back onto the lecture trail, her determination trumping a declining body. In 1867, at about 70 years old, she told the women in the audience at the American Equal Rights Association Annual Meeting to "keep a good faith and good courage," and that "I am going around after I get my business settled and get more equality. People in the North, I am going around to lecture on human rights. I will shake every place I go to."[1]

Over the next 15 years Truth would, indeed, do a lot of "going around and shaking," both across the nation and in her own life. While in Washington working in the contraband camps, she was thrust into confrontations with staff and passengers on the city street cars that helped bring about the integration of public transportation in that city. In the course of the multilayered, multiyear efforts for the contrabands, she worked in the Freedmen's Village camp in Arlington, Virginia, counseling the residents in the proper behaviors of free citizenship and responsible self-support. She then assisted them to find housing and employment outside of Washington, traveling between there, Rochester, New York, Battle Creek, Michigan, and some southern States, making settlement arrangements and accompanying camp dwellers to new homes. Finally, she advanced a solution to the logistical problems of resettling the huge number of camp dwellers on government land in the West. By the early 1870s, she began her lecture tours promoting the western settlement project and gathering petitions to Congress to that end.

In 1867, Truth had moved from Harmonia, Michigan, into the city of Battle Creek, purchasing a barn on an ungraded street that she would fix up into a modest home. It was her last, which she eventually would share with two of her daughters and their children. In 1868 she did more shaking in her personal life by dropping the use of tobacco, a move that she hoped would encourage others to do the same. As she said in two letters to her Rochester friend Amy Post, "My great prayer is that all who smoke may have the spirit that spoke to me to work in them to destroy their desire for tobacco . . . that the seeds of [my] efforts will spread across the whole world."[2] In the next years, she would frequently lecture against the use of tobacco and alcohol, reflecting both her own convictions and also the ferment abroad in the country around temperance.

Social justice for women and their inclusion equally with men in the rights and privileges of citizenship continued to be a concern for Truth. In May of 1870, she spoke at the American Woman Suffrage Association meeting in New York City. She spoke again at a suffrage convention in Hopedale, Massachusetts, in July, and one in Providence, Rhode Island, in October. Truth began adding a critical accent to her

lectures for women's rights, namely a concern about women's style of
dress. Dress reform movements, here and abroad, had been around for
a long time, actually dating to earlier centuries. In the United States,
the National Dress Reform Association was initiated in 1856 as a move
to change the style for proper women's dress. The prevailing fashions
included waist-squeezing corsets, multiple yards of fabric, and several
pounds of petticoats. Reformers believed these were both unhealthy
and unsafe for women, especially if worn while working. The reform
movement pushed a two-layered style that included a dress without a
corset and with a skirt shortened to a few inches below the knee. This
was worn over pants that were very baggy at the top but tapered to a
tight fit around the ankles. Other reformers, such as the Quakers, were
bothered by the extravagance of women's fashions and their frivolous
"worldliness."

This was where Sojourner Truth's concerns lay. Truth had always
lived a very simple life and dressed in the plain, simple style of the
Quakers—a dark-colored dress with a white scarf across her shoulders
and a white cloth wrapped turban-style around her head. For her, bil-
lowing dresses, hairpieces, elaborately constructed hats, and the like,
were, at best, distractions from the more important things of life. Certainly women who supposedly were fighting for reform and women's
rights ought not to be caught up in such things. In one statement,
printed in several newspapers, Truth expressed her irritation and disappointment at "mothers and grey-haired grandmothers [who] wear
high heeled shoes and humps on their heads and put them on their
babies, and stuff them so that they keel over when the wind blows.
Oh mothers, I'm ashamed of ye! What will such lives you live do for
humanity?"[3] Truth was not unique among women's rights reformers
in speaking out critically on dress. Leading women's advocates such
as Elizabeth Smith Miller and Elizabeth Cady Stanton had for years
pushed for dress reform and were promoting the "bloomer dresses"
or "freedom dresses," as they were variously called, for the sake of
women's health and their freedom from clothing that restricted their
movements. But for Truth, the issue was not health. Rather, it was
a question of values: Where should the conscientious person invest
one's time and resources? Material things of decent quality and in

adequate supply were a good thing. But there were higher values that should guide one's life. For her, one should not become "swallowed up in fashionable vanities, spending their time primping instead of praying."[4]

As Truth continued to criss-cross the Midwest, North, and Northeast speaking on the causes that were part of her mission for justice, she found deep satisfaction in the friendships she made and the rich experiences that her travels provided for one who had such humble origins and an early life of enslavement. That is why she carried her Book of Life with her on her journeys. In it she gathered letters and mementos from friends, news clippings reporting on her lectures and public encounters, and the signatures and salutations of meaningful acquaintances made along the way. President Lincoln had written in the Book, as did two later presidents, Ulysses S. Grant and Andrew Johnson. When she was received in the U.S. Senate Chamber in 1870, several members of that body entered their signatures and greetings in the Book, including the celebrated Senator Charles Sumner. While in Massachusetts that year, William Lloyd Garrison signed. During an 1871 visit to her former home, Northampton, Massachusetts, old friends there reflected on the times they had shared and wrote in the Book. Then, stopping by Rochester, New York, in May of that year, she received the signatures of her 20-year acquaintance Amy Post and her cohort on the freedom and justice lecture trail, the esteemed Frederick Douglass. Heading back toward Battle Creek, she was hosted in the home of Mrs. Nannette Gardner, who entered in the Book her distinction as a pathbreaker for women's suffrage, the first female in Michigan to cast a vote in a state election.

Not all things had come up well in Sojourner Truth's life. She had her share of close scrapes with hostile audiences, including verbal and physical abuse by persons who objected to her black presence. There were financial reversals and periods of destitution, among other challenges. Perhaps one of the most difficult moments came for her when her beloved grandson, Sammy Banks, her traveling companion, her reading eyes and writing hands, was stricken with an aneurism during an 1874 trip to Washington, D.C. Retuning to Battle Creek so that he might receive medical care, Truth was forced to face his loss following

Sojourner Truth's gravesite at the Oak Hill Cemetery, Battle Creek, Michigan. Courtesy of the author.

a complex and successful surgery that, nonetheless, was not able ultimately to save his life. Only 24 years old, Sammy held a special a place in her heart, and his death must surely have challenged her personal and faith resources for coping.

Not long thereafter, Truth herself faced a health crisis. She had developed an ulcerative condition on her leg that brought great pain, sapped her strength, and caused her to be bedridden for an extended period of time. To meet her medical expenses she appealed to her friends across the country for assistance. And the contributions came in, from such supporters as antislavery advocates Wendell Phillips, William Lloyd Garrison, and Garrison's son; from a J. Dudley in Richmond, Indiana; and from an Abby May in Boston (quite probably Abby May Alcott, with whom Truth had participated in antislavery activities as early as the 1850s).

By 1876, her condition had improved, to the point that she was ready to travel again, though a journey with friend Frances Titus to the Philadelphia Centennial had to be aborted because of a setback in

Truth's health. But in 1877, Truth and Titus were on the road, traveling through Michigan, with Truth speaking in some 36 towns, especially on temperance. When the 30th anniversary of the first Women's Rights Convention was held in Rochester, New York, in 1878, Truth was one of three Michigan delegates sponsored to the meeting. From July of that year to May of 1879, Truth, accompanied by Titus, spoke at several events in the state. Then, retuning to Battle Creek for long enough to catch her breath, Truth began preparations to travel to Kansas, having learned of the arrival there of the "Exodusters," the mass movement of southern blacks who were emigrating away from the violence and social proscription of their life in the South. Truth had for years thrown herself into the effort to secure a western settlement space for blacks encamped in Washington, D.C. And though the "Colored Exodus" was not the result of her project and involved a different population of blacks than those she sought to help, still she found great excitement in this western development. As she said to a Battle Creek news reporter, "There will be, child, a great glory come out of that. I don't expect I will live to see it. But before this generation has passed away, there will be a grand change. This colored people is going to be a people." Truth and Titus spent the fall of that year working on behalf of the settlers.

Back in Michigan, Sojourner Truth was not done working yet. For the next two years she continued a lecturing agenda in Michigan, Illinois, and Indiana. In March of 1880, Truth lectured to a packed house at the Centennial Hall in Battle Creek. The Battle Creek *Daily Journal* editor related that the audience

> listened, in rapt attention, for over an hour, to the witticisms and brilliant sallies, as they fell from the intuitive mind, through the gifted, inspired lips of this venerable colored orator, who appears to lose none of her wonted originality, vivacity or power, as the years roll on: but is, if possible, more earnest and engaged in whatever good work she undertakes than heretofore.[5]

Truth's subject on this occasion was temperance, which she said she believed was the cause for which her life had been spared. She spoke of her former use of alcohol and tobacco, of how in slavery times owners would freely supply alcohol to their enslaved workers, both at work time and also for funerals, which often led to drunkenness. She offered practical guidance on avoiding the evils of strong drink, especially appealing to young boys not to get caught in the destructive trap of alcohol consumption. In closing her address, Truth reminisced about her days on the antislavery lecture circuit with such persons as William Lloyd Garrison and Wendell Phillips. Then she sang two of her most popular songs "in her peculiar happy strain." The editor complimented Truth on the comprehensiveness and aptness of her remarks, which drew hearty applause from the audience. And he noted especially that the size of the crowd for such a topic and the number of persons who signed on to the temperance pledge was unprecedented, regardless of who had previously been the featured speaker.

The next year, on June 3, 1881, Truth addressed the Michigan Legislature, mainly on the subject of capital punishment. The Battle Creek *Nightly Moon* carried excerpts of her lecture, in which she said,

I have come here tonight to see about a thing that fairly shocked me. It shocked me worse than slavery. I have heard that you are going to have a hanging again in this state. Before God only think of it. When I thought for so many years that I lived in the most blessed state in the union, and then to think of its being made the awful scene of hanging people by the neck until they are dead. Where is the man or woman who can sanction such a thing as that? We are the makers of murderers if we do it. Where do we get this stupid spirit from? Years ago I found out that the religion of Jesus was forgiveness. When I prayed, "Father, forgive me as I forgive those who trespass against me." I found that was against hanging. When a man kills another in cold blood, and you hang him, then you murder in cold blood also. When a prisoner is put into jail to be hung the ministers go to convert him, and they pray that God will forgive him. When he is converted they put a rope around this neck and swing him off; but that is not Jesus' law. But they tell me we must abide by the public laws. I won't sanction any law in my heart that upholds murder. I am against it! I am against it! In olden times it was "an eye for an eye and a tooth for a tooth," but the Savior taught us better things than these, and commanded us to love one another."

Truth related another of her concerns, temperance, to this matter of capital punishment, saying that, "I should like to see you make a law that would hang whiskey out of the United States, for I believe it is at the bottom of a great many crimes. In a great many cases it is not the man that murders, but the whiskey." One cannot say what impact Truth's speech had on the thinking of those present, but apparently her conclusion, if not her reasons, were shared by the majority of the legislature, for after her speech she was informed that the Wyckoff hanging bill, against which she had come to speak, had been defeated. Truth shouted for joy, reaffirmed her belief that Michigan was the most blessed state in the union, and then favored the assembly with the singing of a hymn.[6] In addition to temperance and capital punishment, Truth devoted her remaining lecture engagements to appeals for prison reform and also for workers' rights.

The Sojourner Truth Monument in Battle Creek, dedicated in 1999, features a bronze sculpture of Truth by Tina Allen. Courtesy of the author.

INTO THE SUNSET—"WITH HER BOOTS ON"

By the early 1880s, when Truth herself was in her eighties, she presented a dual image to the world. On the one hand, her increasing physical limitations caused her to pare back her travel and lecture schedule. She had long depended on the use of a cane, as a result of injuries by a hostile mob at one of her speaking engagements. But now both her hearing and her sight were failing, and the ulcers on her leg continued to bring her pain and periodic incapacitation. On the other hand, on those occasions when she appeared in public or received visitors to her home, she exhibited a level of physical vigor and incisive clarity of thought that continued to astound those who conversed with her. For instance, in March of 1880, Frances Titus organized a surprise party for Truth. It was attended by some 60 persons, including the women of the Woman's Christian Temperance Union. The guests provided a sumptuous meal, bouquets of flowers, an original poetic reading, and eager listening ears to the sage woman's casual conversation. The news report of the event said that "No one who listened will ever forget the quaint sayings that fell like apples of gold from her inspired lips,—words of wisdom and truth, crisp aphorisms, that have made Sojourner Truth the remarkable woman she has become." Truth sang "in a deep and sonorous voice" "There Is a Home Beyond" and "There Is a Bright Celestial City." And then, according to the editor: "Her hair that a few years ago was snowy white has turned back to its natural black color."[7]

In an undated article appearing in the Battle Creek *Journal*, probably in early 1883, the writer, a Carli D. Beach, recounts his visit to Truth's home, in fulfillment of a promise made to her the previous fall. He noted her still lively sense of humor, as when she said she suffered from a "sort o' room a tisum," a pun she was making on her having to be virtually confined to her room. She could still make her own bed and putter around the house a bit, but her daughters, who were living with her, took care of cooking and household maintenance. Yet, said Beach, though the curls in her hair were "taking on the frost of age," "her second sight and hearing are still perfect," and he found her "nearly as fresh and free from wrinkles as in the days of childhood." As to her mind, he found remarkable her "well preserved faculties" and her "sound sense and ready wit."

Back in 1881, Sojourner Truth had expressed her confident anticipa-
tion of attending the 1883 World's Fair scheduled to be held in Chicago.
It was not to be, however. By July of 1883, Truth was suffering badly
from the ulcers on her legs that had now spread to her arms. Seeing the
grave state of her condition, her friend Dr. John Harvey Kellogg admitted her to his highly reputed Battle Creek Sanitarium (then known as
the Western Reform Health Institute), where the staff could provide
for her constant care. Dr. Kellogg was devoted to Truth. To heal one of
her ulcers he reportedly grafted skin from his own arm onto her leg. But
other sores were too far advanced. Returned to her home on College
Street, she yet received visitors and asked of her friends that they purchase her pictures of her house, as she still "sells the shadow to support
the substance." The sanitarium doctors came each day to monitor her
condition. Comfort and support were provided by her daughters Diana
and Elizabeth, and by her trusted friend Frances Titus.

*Dr. John Harvey Kellogg, chief physician at the famed
Battle Creek Sanitarium, who admired Sojourner Truth
and treated her leg ulcers toward the end of her life.
Courtesy of the Willard Library, Battle Creek, Michigan.*

As one might expect from the depth and integrity of her religious faith, Sojourner Truth embraced her eminent transition from this life with calm and grace. She dictated her will and signed it with her X. She requested a clergyperson whom she had long known and respected, the Rev. Samuel J. Rogers, to deliver her eulogy. A visit from a friend on November 24, two days before she passed, found her weakened and emaciated and able to speak only a little. When she did speak, it was mostly about her faith in the God who had come to her and who, even then, she said, "speaks through me in a wonderful way." This God "is in all, and his glory is beautiful." Rather than to be feared, "Death," she said, "is an everlasting step, and we must look for no end." Though her speech was halting, said the visitor, "her mind seems as bright as ever"; she recounted accurately conversations that had occurred 15 years prior. Over the protest of her daughters, Truth sang a hymn for her visitor. As he took his leave, she bid him goodbye, with the closing appeal, "Be a follower of Jesus."[8]

In the spirit that had characterized her entire life, in the exuberant confidence in the future before her, and with the same flair for cutting repartee that saw her through decades of public lectures, Sojourner Truth, the would-be object of consolation, herself consoled one of her final visitors who referred to her eminent death, with "I'm not going to die, honey; I'm going home like a shooting star."[9] At 3 A.M., Monday, November 26, 1883, her star blazed across the midwestern sky, on its homeward journey. And what might she expect when she arrived? The sojourning lecturer for justice and rights told an audience on her initial visit to Battle Creek, in 1856, "I believe in the next world. When we gets up yonder, we shall have all of the rights 'stored to us again—all that love what I've lost—all going to be 'stored to me again. Oh! How good God is!"[10]

NOTES

1. Manning Marable, *Freedom on My Mind* (New York: Columbia University Press, 2003), p. 8.

2. Copies of letters, one January 18, 1869, another undated, found in the Willard Library, Helen Warner Branch, Battle Creek, MI.

3. Sojourner Truth Institute, http://www.sojournertruth.org/Library/Speeches/Default.htm#DRESS; also quoted in Suzanne Pullon Fitch

and Roseann M. Mandziuk, *Sojourner Truth As Orator* (Westport, CT: Greenwood Press, 1997), p. 45.

4. Carleton Mabee, *Sojourner Truth: Slave, Prophet, Legend* (New York: New York University Press, 1993), p. 192.

5. March 7, 1880.

6. Speech excerpts quoted in Marable, *Freedom on My Mind*, pp. 394–95; see also Sojourner Truth Institute, http://www.sojourner truth.org/Library/Speeches/Default.htm#PUNISHMENT.

7. Article reprint found in the Willard Library, Helen Warner Branch, journal name not given. An abbreviated account appeared in the Michigan *Tribune*, March 6, 1880; reprint also in the Willard Library, Warner Branch.

8. Battle Creek *Nightly Moon*, November 24, 1883, reprint found in the Willard Library, Warner Branch.

9. W. Terry Whalin, *Sojourner Truth: American Abolitionist* (Urichsville, OH: Barbour & Company, 1997), p. 193.

10. Sojourner Truth Institute, http://www.sojournertruth.org/Library/Speeches/Default.htm.

POSTSCRIPT: LOOKING BACK ACROSS THE VALLEY

Two days after her death, Sojourner Truth's funeral was held at the Congregational-Presbyterian Church in Battle Creek, in fulfillment of her wishes. Nearly a thousand people followed the black-plumed hearse from her home to the church. Friends and coworkers in the various rights causes she had championed celebrated her for the public and personal witness of her life. The eulogy was delivered by the Rev. Reed Stuart. She was buried in Battle Creek's Oak Hill Cemetery, next to her beloved grandson Samuel Banks.

Sojourner Truth, born Isabella Bomefree, began her public career at some 46 years of age, a time when most people of her time were beginning to think about slowing down. Making a transition from domestic worker whose skills and efficiency were highly valued to a traveling evangelist, Truth was one of the few women in the public speaking arena in the 19th century. Indeed, the mores of the day considered women's assertion of themselves in public to be contrary both to their natural abilities and to their appropriate role as women.

As a thinker and a speaker, Truth took a "zero-based" approach to her social reality. That is to say, her assessments of reality were not filtered through arbitrary value constructions or bound by social convention. Instead, she interrogated societal givens by her own value standards of "mother wit"—common, intuitive good sense—by the tenets of her own faith, and by her own standards of justice and equity. Thus, she could walk away, literally, from her legal obligation to her owner Dumont, enforceable by the state as she knew it to be, because in her view he had been unfair. Further, Truth could assess religious ideas, including religious innovations, such as Spiritualism and Millerite thought, on their own terms, rather than on the pronouncements of church authorities. She could critique them where they didn't make sense to her. Likewise, she could challenge long-held, orthodox theological tenets, as when she publicly declared that she no longer believed there was a hell of eternal punishment, since this was not consistent with her view of a gracious God. Though she could not read, Truth was very familiar with the textual source upon which Christians based religious authority, the Bible. She knew it well and could quote from it extensively. She did not trust others' interpretations of the scriptures, though; she wanted to hear them read word for word, without comment, so that she could discern her own sense of the message of God that the text was attempting to convey. She even longed for the day when someone would redraft the scriptures and edit out the offensive sections, those that did not reflect the will and the way of an inclusive, loving God.

Thus, throughout her life, Truth was an "equal opportunity" iconoclast: no issue was outside the scope of her advocacy for truth, justice, and, what she grew to value and affirm, the American Way of constitutional political and juridical governance. Hence, she was a leading voice for abolition, for all the enslaved; she was a consistent voice for debunking the assumptions about women's worth and abilities and for eliminating the consequent social constrictions on them. She spoke out against the exploitation of the poor and marginalized, whatever their racial or ethnic identity; against socially disruptive substance abuse; against the inhumaneness and theological error of capital punishment.

For Sojourner Truth, the righting of social wrongs was not a quest for personal advancement. Her claim that she could compete more than favorably with men in physical tasks, yet, "Ar'n't I a woman," was not an appeal for personal access to male privileges. Instead, she was offering herself as representative of the *class* of womanhood, a class that merited reassessment through fair, unbiased eyes, rather than through preconceived notions about who they were or of what they were capable. It was a challenge to the premises of male dominance and female subjugation, rather than simply to their ad hoc practice.

A basic religious faith instilled by her parents, recast and given personal passion by a conversion experience, established the prism through which she would view every aspect of the world and her place in it. When she became disillusioned with life in New York City, she set out on an evangelistic mission, to share with others her experiential encounter with God and to invite them into the same relationship with God that she now treasured. She was going forth to "lecture" for this holy cause. But her interactions with prominent 19th-century reformers, occasioned by her chance residence in a reformers community, led her to see that spiritual transformation and social transformation were but complementary aspects of the same holy cause. Thus, a native sense of justice and equity, given purposive framing by a passionate faith, and informed by an extended knowledge of the social conditions, set her on a mission to reconcile the contradictions of human abuse and oppression that had become domesticated in U.S. society. She was convinced that this was God's intention for her life and that God would guide and sustain her through to the accomplishment of her mission. This assurance shielded her from despair in the face of setback and from fear in the presence of formidable foes.

There could be a blunt invectiveness to Truth's words and sentiments. For instance, she publicly criticized the women of a women's rights meeting who, in the style of the day, were attired "with goose-wings on your heads, as if you were going to fly, and dressed in such ridiculous fashion."[1] She spoke of the government agents at the contraband camps in Washington, D.C., as those who were stealing for themselves the "loaves and fishes" intended for the people and leaving them only the "scales and crusts."[2] When the national administration, seeing the reversals of fortune of the all-white Union army, finally opened military enlistment to blacks, Truth's response was that it was just like in slavery, black folks were always called in to clean up the mess of white folks.

But there was also an inclusive graciousness to Sojourner Truth's spirit. Slavery had been for her an odious experience. She recounted its horrors to audiences throughout her speaking career. Yet, she often also told audiences that her campaign against slavery was almost as much to save white people from going to hell for their perpetration as it was to relieve the earthly suffering of their enslaved victims. (Though she later disavowed a belief in a literal Hell, she continued to see blacks as instruments of God for the redemption of white people.) And she could extend a generous reception to her former owner, Dumont, when they met after her self-manumission, and accept his remorseful repentance in later years for his participation in the slavery system.

Perhaps this broadness of spirit was the natural outflow of her take on religious faith. In her youth, her parents had told her of a God who was in the heavens and was available to her wherever she went and under whatever circumstances she found herself. This sketch of the divine was unsupported by regular religious instruction and spiritual nurture, since her owners were not devoted to the church nor did they provide for the religious oversight of their chattel laborers. As Truth grew to adulthood, she carried a conception of God as "a great man, like Napoleon Bonaparte or George Washington," whose relevance was only as a rescuing helper in time of trouble. But following her conversion experience, and as her faith matured, she came to a more expansive conception of God, as one who pervaded the universe and had care for all of creation. All is from God, who is without beginning or end, she said. God is "a great ocean of love; and we live and move in Him as the fishes in the sea, filled with His love and spirit, and His throne is in the hearts of people." "We are all children of one Father . . . who is no respecter of persons." And though God is ever present, "We shall never see God, only as we see Him in one another."[3] With such a religious perspective, Truth could be open to all people and could find grounds for mutuality in human striving and ultimate reconciliation in human conflict.

Truth had unyielding confidence in her God, whom she credited with compensating for her illiteracy. What others derived from the printed word, she said, God revealed to her directly. "God Himself talks to me," she would say. Thus, she believed that while others could read books, she could "read people and nations."

Truth was a motivational speaker par excellence. The learned, the highly cultured, the common laborer, even the ruffian, all fell under the spell of her oratory. As her social prophetic vision took shape and began to infuse itself into her lectures, leaders in social justice movements recognized in her a powerful, effective spokesperson, and she began receiving invitations to represent those movements in public meetings.

Truth's critical insights and her ability to convey those with passion, disarming genuineness, and guileless but inventively clever phrasing made her a very popular speaker, whether on the docket of conventions and organizational events or at lectures that she scheduled for herself. Her speeches were typically the most memorable of the several that might be offered on a given occasion, as news journals show, not least because of her art and skill at handling naysayers and hecklers, a frequent presence in rights meetings. Another key element must be mentioned, though: song. Whether her own compositions, of which there were many, or existing published numbers, Truth frequently interjected music into public and private gatherings. Audiences craved to hear her robust, vibrant, affective singing. She would incorporate it into her presentations. When a meeting or event had no music scheduled, she would offer some songs on her own. It was not uncommon for the announcement of a program on which she was to speak to include Truth's singing as part of the attraction.

Making the argument for a social cause and inspiring listeners to act were Truth's fortes. But it seems she was not a movement organizer or strategist. Her petition drive for a western land allotment for black resettlement was not highly structured or coordinated. Nor does it appear that she functioned in the decision-making counsels of the abolitionists, of women's suffragists, or of other causes. She was not without the drive or the ability to carry through structured tasks. After all, in her working days, she was highly regarded for her efficiency and productivity: she pursued and won three separate court suits, and she coordinated some operational services in the Washington camps and effected the relocation to other states of many of the people in them. But her penchant seems to have been toward individual initiative in stirring up the gifts of audiences and providing them the ideational and motivational resources to act. And this she did exceedingly well. She left to others the nuts and bolts tasks of organizational development and institutional maintenance.

Perhaps this operational mode was appropriate for one who was a "sojourner," one who resides in one place temporarily. Throughout her adult life in freedom, Truth was continually on the move, lodging with friends or with the strangers who took her in, either according to the practices of hospitality of that day or because they invited her as an honored guest. She was on a mission, a communication/agitation mission, and the technology of the times, her inability to write, and the desire for maximal effectiveness required her to go to where the word needed to be heard. Without family obligations to constrain her, and with the urgency of her vocation impelling her, she went. Though she longed for a home of her own, a symbolic and actual physical anchor point for her life, she did not stay there long when that was achieved. The homes she purchased in Northampton, Massachusetts, and later in the Battle Creek, Michigan, area, mainly served as rest stops on her peripatetic journeying.

And a long journey of many byways it was, undoubtedly with dead ends and detours, serendipities, and, surely in Truth's perspective, divine interventions, along the way. The Rev. Samuel Rodgers tells of one such, however one classifies it:

> It was during the dark days of 1863 that she [Truth] became ill and despondent. She was quite destitute and thought she was about to die, and hence made a special request that I should preach her funeral sermon. I assured her that I would be willing to do so as she requested, but said: "I don't think you had better die just yet. Don't you want to see all your people free? The best thing you can do is to get well so that you can live to see this war ended and the slaves free. Much more was said and I found in a day or two that cheery words had been better than medicine. The woman improved rapidly and found before the close of the war that there was much work for her to do.

And work she did, for 20 more years.

Sojourner Truth was a remarkable woman by any measure. The unsolicited accolades and tributes to her moral, spiritual, oratorical, physical, and personal giftedness, from persons of all classes and social stripes, bear ample testimony to this assessment. The editor of the Detroit *Advertiser* said that she "had a heart of love" and "a tongue of fire." Another news editor, in encouraging public attendance at one of her upcoming lectures, wrote,

> The lecturer is a child of nature, gifted beyond the common measure . . . with an open, broad honesty of heart, and unbounded kindness. Wholly untaught in the schools, she is herself a study for the philosophers, and a wonder to all. Her natural powers of observation, discrimination, comparison, and intuition are rare, indeed, and only equaled by her straightforward commonsense and earnest practical benevolence."[4]

Frederick Douglass's tribute, sent upon news of her death, was that she was "venerable for age, distinguished for insight into human nature, remarkable for independence and courageous self-assertion."[5]

Subsequent generations have continued to honor the historical contributions of Sojourner Truth to U.S. life and culture. The citizens of Battle Creek have erected a major monument to her in a downtown plaza of that city and named a section of highway after her. She has been inducted into the National and Michigan Women's Halls of Fame. A U.S. postage stamp bears her image, and the National Aeronautics and Space Administration named its Mars Pathfinder landrover Sojourner. But perhaps the most fitting benediction for a woman who believed that women could "turn right side up" again a toppled human community of injustice was the word offered at her death by her hometown Battle Creek *Journal*, in fact giving honor to a prophet in her own country:

> No longer a literal "sojourner" on this earthly sphere in bodily form, her name will still remain engraven upon the grateful memory of the millions of her countrymen for whose freedom and welfare she has labored, and upon the monument of human remembrance which can never perish.[6]

NOTES

1. Frances Titus, *Narrative of Sojourner Truth; A Bondswoman of Olden Time, with a History of Her Labors and Correspondence Drawn from Her "Book of Life"* (Battle Creek, MI: Published by the author, 1878), p. 243.

2. Erlene Stetson and Linda David, *Glorying in Tribulation: The Life-work of Sojourner Truth* (East Lansing: Michigan State University Press, 1994), p. 4.

3. *A.M.E. Christian Recorder*, February 3, 1881.

4. Titus, *Narrative of Sojourner Truth*, p. 227.

5. W. Terry Whalin, *Sojourner Truth: American Abolitionist* (Uhrichs-ville, OH: Barbour & Company, 1997), p. 194.

6. November 26, 1883, quoted in Martin L. Ashley, "Frances Titus: Sojourner's Trusted Scribe." http://www.sojournertruth.org/Library/Archive/Titus-TrustedScribe.htm.

SELECTED BIBLIOGRAPHY

EDITIONS OF *NARRATIVE OF SOJOURNER TRUTH*

Gilbert, Olive, ed. *Narrative of Sojourner Truth, A Northern Slave*. Boston: J. B. Yerrington and Son, Printers, 1850.
The first published Sojourner Truth biography, edited by friend Gilbert, to whom Truth dictated her life story up to that point in time.

Titus, Frances, ed. *Narrative of Sojourner Truth; A Bondswoman of Olden Time, with a History of her Labors and Correspondence Drawn from Her "Book of Life."* Battle Creek, MI: Published by the author, 1878.
Titus, Truth's trusted friend and traveling companion in her later years, adds details of Truth's life after the 1850 Gilbert *Narrative*, including excerpts from Truth's "Book of Life" scrapbook of autographs, news clippings, and historical artifacts.

Washington, Margaret, ed. *Narrative of Sojourner Truth*. New York: Vintage Classics, 1993.

This edition offers an introduction to the 1850 Gilbert biography, providing helpful background information and insights on Truth's historical times and how she met the issues of her day.

CORE SOJOURNER TRUTH BIBLIOGRAPHY

Fauset, Arthur Huff. *Sojourner Truth, God's Faithful Pilgrim*. Chapel Hill: University of North Carolina Press, 1944.
Seeks to illumine what the author sees as the healthy balance in African American religious piety between conscientious adherence to divine moral dictates and living a responsibly liberated life of joy. Truth's life story is offered as exemplary of this.

Mabee, Carleton, with Susan Mabee Newhouse. *Sojourner Truth: Slave, Prophet, Legend*. New York: New York University Press, 1993.
Extensively documented treatment of Truth's life. Authors attempt to separate, in their judgment, fact from myth and legend in the accounts of the events of Truth's life.

McKissack, Patricia C., and Frederick McKissack. *Sojourner Truth: Ain't I a Woman?* New York: Scholastic, 1992.
This is one of several written especially for juvenile readers.

Painter, Nell Irvin. *Sojourner Truth: A Life, A Symbol*. New York: W. W. Norton, 1996.
Noted author examines the variety of sources on Truth's life in an attempt to reveal its meaning and impact on her times, as well as for the present.

Pauli, Hertha. *Her Name Was Sojourner Truth*. New York: Appleton-Century-Crofts, 1962.
A very appreciative retelling of the main currents in Truth's life, cast in engaging, literary prose. Adds rich detail that gives color and vibrance to the narrative.

Rockwell, Anne F. *Only Passing Through: The Story of Sojourner Truth*. New York: Random House, 2000.
A picture book biography by a highly regarded storyteller and widely published author of children's stories.

Sillen, Samuel. *Women against Slavery*. New York: Masses & Mainstream, 1955.

Places Truth in the context of 19th-century women who were actively involved in movements for abolition and women's rights.

Stetson, Erlene, and Linda David. *Glorying in Tribulation: The Lifework of Sojourner Truth*. East Lansing: Michigan State University Press, 1994.

A thoughtful new interpretation of Truth's life and historical impact, based on solid research and careful analysis of the sources.

Stewart, Jeffrey C., ed. *Narrative of Sojourner Truth: A Bondswoman of Olden Time, with a History of Her Labors and Correspondence Drawn from her "Book of Life."* New York: Oxford University Press, 1991.

A reissue of Frances Titus, ed. *Narrative of Sojourner Truth; A Bondswoman of Olden Time, with a History of her Labors and Correspondence Drawn from Her "Book of Life,"* in which Stewart provides an Introduction setting Truth's contributions as a commanding 19th-century voice for justice causes, especially abolitionism and women's rights, in the context of her millennialist Christian faith, while noting the interjections into the picture we have received of Truth's life and message of the views of persons such as Francis Gage, who left the written records by which Truth is known. Still, asserts Stewart, the core of Truth's voice and message survive intact as a remarkable legacy to the present.

FURTHER READING

Accomando, Christina. *The Regulations of Robbers: Legal Fictions of Slavery and Resistance*. Columbus: Ohio State University Press, 2001.

Alexander, Amy. *Fifty Black Women Who Changed America*. New York: Citadel Press, 1999.

American Equal Rights Association. *Proceedings of the First Anniversary of the American Equal Rights Association*. Held at the Church of the Puritans, New York, May 9 and 10, 1867. New York: R. J. Johnston, 1867.

Andrews, William L. *Classic African American Women's Narratives*. Oxford: Oxford University Press, 2003.

Aptheker, Herbert. *A Documentary History of the Negro People in the United States*. Vol. 2. New York: Citadel Press, 1970.

Asher, Sandra F. *A Woman Called Truth: A Play in Two Acts Celebrating the Life of Sojourner Truth*. Woodstock, IL: Dramatic Publishing, 1993.

Baker, Jean H., ed. *Votes for Women: The Struggle for Suffrage Revisited*. Oxford: Oxford University Press, 2002.

Bennett, Michael. *Democratic Discourses: The Radical Abolition Movement and Antebellum American Literature*. New Brunswick, NJ: Rutgers University Press, 2005.

Bernard, Jacqueline. *Journey toward Freedom: The Story of Sojourner Truth*. New York: Norton & Company, 1967.

Carter, H. "Sojourner Truth." *The Chautauquan: A Weekly Magazine*, May, 1887. American Periodicals Series Online. http://www. columbia.edu/cu/lweb/eresources/databases/2803564.html.

Chmielewski, Wendy E. "Sojourner Truth: Utopian Vision and Search for Community, 1797–1883." In *Women in Spiritual and Communitarian Societies in the United States*, ed. W. E. Chmielewski, L. J. Kern, and M. Klee-Hartzell, 21–37. New York: Syracuse University Press, 1993.

Conboy, Katie. *Writing on the Body: Female Embodiment and Feminist Theory*. New York: Columbia University Press, 1997.

Cotton, M. Jeanne Dolphus. "Bethune, Truth, Tubman Profile Contrast." Master's thesis, Garrett-Evangelical Theological Seminary, Evanston, IL, 1979.

DeLombard, Jeannine Marie. *Slavery on Trial: Law, Abolitionism, and Print Culture*. Chapel Hill: University of North Carolina Press, 2007.

Fitch, Suzanne Pullon, and Roseann M. Mandziuk. *Sojourner Truth as Orator: Wit, Story, and Song*. Westport, CT: Greenwood Press, 1997.

Foss, K. A. "Sojourner Truth Antislavery and Women's Rights Lecturer." In *American Orators before 1900: Critical Studies and Sources*, ed. B. K. Duffy and H. R. Ryan, 385–90. New York: Greenwood Press, 1987.

Fulton, Doveanna S. *Speaking Power: Black Feminist Orality in Women's Narratives of Slavery*. New York: State University of New York Press, 2006.

Gottheimer, Josh, ed. *Ripples of Hope: Great American Civil Rights Speeches*. New York: Basic Civitas Books, 2003.

Haynes, Elizabeth Ross. *Unsung Heroes*. New York: Du Bois and Dill Publishers, 1921.

Hopkins, Pauline Elizabeth. *Daughter of the Revolution: The Major Nonfiction Works of Pauline E. Hopkins*. New Brunswick, NJ: Rutgers University Press, 2007.

Lee, Valerie, ed. *The Prentice Hall Anthology of African American Women's Literature*. Upper Saddle River, NJ: Pearson Prentice Hall, 2006.

Lunsford, Andrea A. *Reclaiming Rhetorica: Women in the Rhetorical Tradition*. Pittsburgh: University of Pittsburgh Press, 1995.

Manning, Marable, ed. *Freedom on My Mind*. The Columbia Documentary History of the African American Experience. New York: Columbia University Press, 2003.

Montgomery, Janey W. *A Comparative Analysis of the Rhetoric of Two Negro Women Orators—Sojourner Truth and Frances E. Watkins Harper*. Hays: Fort Hays Kansas State College, 1968.

Ortiz, Victoria. *Sojourner Truth, a Self-Made Woman*. Philadelphia: J. B. Lippincott Company, 1974.

Painter, Nell Irvin. "Sojourner Truth." In *The American Radical*, ed. Mari Jo Buhle, Paul Buhle and Harvey J. Kaye, 25–31. New York: Routledge, 1994.

Peterson, Carla L. *Doers of the Word: African-American Women Speakers and Writers in the North (1830–1880)*. Oxford: Oxford University Press, 1995.

Sitomer, Alan, and Michael Cirelli. *Hip-Hop Poetry and the Classics*. Beverly Hills, CA: Milk Mug Publishing, 2004.

Smith, Jessie Carney, ed. *Notable Black American Women*. Detroit: Gale Research, 1992.

Turner, Morrie, and Letha Turner. *Famous Black Americans*. Valley Forge, PA: Judson Press, 1973.

United States Senate. *An Act to Direct the Joint Committee on the Library to Accept the Donation of a Bust Depicting Sojourner Truth and to*

Display the Bust in a Suitable Location in the Capital. Washington, DC: U.S. Government Printing Office, 2006.

Wagner-Martin, Linda, and Cathy N. Davidson, eds. *The Oxford Book of Women's Writing in the United States.* Oxford: Oxford University Press, 1995.

Walker, Robbie J. "Sojourner Truth: Lecturer, Abolitionist, Women's Rights Speaker." In *African American Orators: A Bio-Critical Sourcebook,* ed. R. W. Leeman, 332–40. Westport, CT: Greenwood Press, 1996.

Whalin, W. Terry. *Sojourner Truth: American Abolitionist.* Uhrichsville, OH: Barbour & Company, 1997.

Wideman, John Edgar, ed. *My Soul Has Grown Deep: Classics of Early African-American Literature.* Philadelphia: Running Press, 2001.

Wilson-Logan, Shirley. *With Pen and Voice: A Critical Anthology of Nineteenth-Century African-American Women.* Carbondale: Southern Illinois University Press, 1995.

INTERNET SOURCES

http://www.sojournertruth.org/. Includes a library of historical documents, photos, speeches, and other materials by and about Sojourner Truth.About.com: Women's History, http://womensh istory.about.com/od/howejwriting/a/mothers_day.htm

Answers.com. "When Woman Gets Her Rights Man will be Right," http://www.answers.com/topic/when-woman-gets-her-rights-man-will-be-right-c-1860-by-sojourner-truth

Cornell University Law School. Legal Information Institute, http://topics.law.cornell.edu/constitution/amendmentxiv

The National Archives. The Freedmen's Bureau, 1865–72, http://www.archives.gov/research/african-americans/freedmens-bureau/

Papers Past, http://paperspast.natlib.govt.nz/cgi-bin/paperspast?a=d&cl=search&d=WCT18680829.2.23&srpos=13&e=————10—11—on—2%22strange+creature%22-article.

The Rise and Fall of Jim Crow, http://www.pbs.org/wnet/jimcrow/stories_events_freed.html

"Women in History," http://www.lkwdpl.org/wihohio/keck-eli.htm

NEWSPAPERS AND JOURNALS

A.M.E. Christian Recorder, February 3, 1881.

"George Thompson in Rochester," *Antislavery Bugle,* May 17, 1851, p. 3.

"Lecture by Sojourner Truth," New York *Tribune,* November 8, 1853, p. 6.

"Sojourner Truth," Chicago *Daily Inter Ocean,* August 13, 1879, p. 3.

"Women's Rights Convention," New York *Herald,* October 25, p. 1

"Women's Rights Convention," New York *Herald,* October 28, 1850, p. 3.

"Women's Rights Convention," New York *Tribune,* October 26, 1850, pp. 5–6.

LIBRARIES AND RESEARCH COLLECTIONS

Periodicals and Newspapers Reading Room, Northwestern University, Evanston, IL.

Willard Library, Helen Warner Branch, Battle Creek, MI.

INDEX

About the Author

LARRY G. MURPHY is Professor of the History of Christianity at Garrett-Evangelical Theological Seminary in Evanston, Illinois. He is the author of *African American Faith in America*, the editor of *Down by the Riverside: Readings in African American Religion*, and co-editor of the *Encyclopedia of African American Religions*.